D0727872

Introduction

Classical music CDs are now being issued at such a rate that nobody can possibly keep track of what's around. Just a glance at the catalogue reveals that practically every work by the major composers has been recorded, often several times over – to say nothing of the hundreds of obscurities keeping company with the household names. To make matters worse, the stores tend to concentrate on the latest heavily promoted recordings, so while the catalogue might tell you that you can choose between ninety different versions of Vivaldi's *Four Seasons*, to the uninitiated it can seem there's not much choice at all. If you're a newcomer to classical music, or could just do with some help in making sense of the huge array of recordings, the **Rough Guide to 100 Essential Classical CDs** is what you need.

This book is not a tally of the 100 "greatest" pieces of music – any such list would be meaningless. Rather, these 100 recordings comprise a collection of great CDs which together give an overview of the whole range of classical music, from the twelfth century to the work of contemporaries as dissimilar as Pierre Boulez and Arvo Pärt. The biggest names – composers such as Bach, Mozart, Beethoven and Stravinsky – are represented by several discs; less prominent figures have been allocated fewer, in some instances sharing a CD with another – Borodin, for example, features on the same disc as Smetana. In all instances, the aim is the same: to introduce the best of each composer's music, through interpretations of the highest calibre.

The composers are arranged alphabetically, with multiple-work entries being arranged in ascending order of scale from small to large – so that, for example, Beethoven's entries begin with a disc of piano sonatas and culminate with his colossal *Symphony No. 9*. There's a wide range of different genres on display, with a profusion of symphonies, concertos and string quartets, but one genre, opera, is absent – it's covered in a companion volume, the *Rough Guide to 100 Essential Opera CDs*. When it comes to the question of old recordings versus new, our selection is as even-handed as possible: the earliest recording in the book (Brahms's *Clarinet Quintet*) first appeared in 1937, while the latest (Monteverdi's *Vespers*) was released in 1999. Past performers are not necessarily the best, as some nostalgists maintain: the young pianist Yevgeny Kissin, or the violinist Anne-Sophie Mutter, are outstanding by any standards. Conversely, to demand modern technology and only listen to digital recordings is to cut yourself off from a wealth of marvellous material. In many cases so-called "historical" recordings had excellent sound in the first place, and remastering can work wonders in freshening up a performance. On the one or two occasions that a recording clearly sounds its age we have said so, and given reasons why the insights of that particular performance justify the CD's inclusion.

All our recommendations are currently available in Europe and North America, although some may require a special order. Every review is illustrated with the cover of the current edition, but bear in mind that classical music is re-packaged and re-released so frequently that some of our CDs may re-emerge in different form before too long. So if you can't find what you're looking for, get your stockist to check if it has been re-issued with a new catalogue number – it's extremely unlikely that any of the brilliant performances in this book will ever become extinct.

Acknowledgements

Many people contributed with help and advice to this book. Thanks are due to the record companies for supplying material and information; to Anne Hegerty for proofreading; Anna Wray for typesetting; Lewes Music Library for their customary efficiency; Nicolas Bloomfield for his suggestions; Matthew Boyden for his assistance; and to Jonathan Buckley for his patience as an editor. I would also like to thank my mother – to whom this book is dedicated – and, finally, Rebecca Meitlis for her discerning ears, which have steered me away from the obvious on many an occasion.

Joe Staines

Johann Sebastian Bach

Goldberg Variations

Glenn Gould (piano)

Sony SMK 52619; mid-price

No classical music recording of the last twenty years has aroused such passions as Glenn Gould's 1981 account of Bach's *Goldberg Variations*. For the Canadian pianist's many admirers, it is a near-definitive interpretation and the summation of his achievements as the supreme Bach pianist of the post-war period. To his critics, it is mannered to the point of eccentricity, not least because of the extreme speeds employed and the pianist's distracting habit of tunelessly humming along as he plays. In fact it's perfectly possible to maintain both positions and to celebrate Gould's reading as an example of a forceful and idiosyncratic performer successfully imposing his musical personality onto a great masterpiece.

Bach's own renown in his lifetime was achieved, primarily, through his consummate skill as a keyboard player and improviser, and the *Goldberg Variations* represent one of his supreme achievements as a composer for the harpsichord. This set of thirty variations on a theme was supposedly commissioned by Baron von Keyserling – the Russian Ambassador to the Dresden court – in order to relieve his insomnia, and was named after the baron's harpsichordist who was to play them. The work begins with a highly ornamented but rather demure theme (a Sarabande played with a rapt deliberation in this recording) around whose bass line Bach then proceeds to fashion an astonishing series of transformations.

The variations are in groups of three with the third of the group a canon – that is, a melody stated by two or more "voices", each beginning slightly after the preceding one. This interweaving of different strands of sound – known as counterpoint – is intricate and technical stuff, but it was second nature to Bach and in his hands it always sounds vibrantly alive rather than artificial or mechanical. The pattern of canons is only broken in the very last variation – a rousing, festive conclusion in which Bach brilliantly combines two popular German folk songs in a manner known as a quodlibet. The whole work feels epic in scope not just because of its length, but also because of its enormous variety – there are variations with the pomp of a French overture, some which suggest the human voice, and yet others which feel like pure display pieces. In terms of mood the variations, similarly, range far and wide, and yet with the underlying presence of the original thematic material – sometimes discernible, sometimes not – binding the whole work together. When the original theme is re-stated after the final variation, it feels like returning home after a long journey.

Gould's approach to playing Baroque harpsichord music on a piano is certainly very different from that of Murray Perahia (see p.142). There's a definite suggestion of the harpsichord's crispness of attack in his playing which is characterized, in particular, by a vivid precision of touch. Each line of counterpoint is always clearly articulated but frequently in different ways. Everything seems calculated to present the internal complexity of the music as sharply as possible – pedalling is minimal and there are no blurry edges. Compared to Gould's 1955 debut recording of the same work, which stirred up even more argument than this one, the 1981 recording has far more gravitas. He explained his later approach as follows: "the music that moves me very deeply is music that I want to hear played or want to play myself . . . in a very ruminative, very deliberate tempo." On one level it's as if he aspires to a kind of objectivity, and yet at the same time Gould's playing is utterly personal – in each of the variations you can sense the thought behind every note.

Johann Sebastian Bach

Suites for Violoncello Solo

Anner Bylsma (cello)

Sony S2K 48 047; full price

Bach's genius at the keyboard perhaps explains why he wrote relatively few works for other solo instruments. Nearly all that he did write dates from the period 1717–21, when he was composer to Prince Leopold of Anhalt-Cöthen. The finest of these are the six suites for unaccompanied cello, and the partitas and sonatas for unaccompanied violin, works which push the expressive and technical possibilities of their instruments to unprecedented extremes.

Although a stringed instrument is capable of playing two notes at the same time, what one expects to hear, when it's played on its own, is a single line of music. Bach's *Cello Suites* certainly abound in simple uncomplicated melodies – in each suite's penultimate movement for example – but there are many movements where a multi-textured sound is created that is able to suggest a harmonic underpinning and even, on one occasion, a fugue. A spectacular example of this is the Prelude of the first suite, in which successive chords are not played as such but are separated out into their individual notes – what you hear is both the gently rocking, forward momentum of the separated notes, and the implicit harmony underneath.

In each of the suites Bach employs an almost identical arrangement of movements. To the basic core of the traditional Baroque suite – slow Allemande, flowing Courante, stately Sarabande and lively Gigue – he adds an opening Prelude and a pair of dainty French dances: Minuets in *No. 1* and *No. 2*, Bourrées in *No. 3* and *No. 4*, and Gavottes in *No. 5* and *No. 6*. The greatest freedom of expression is found in the Preludes which take the form of improvisatory fantasies around broken chords and scale-like passages. The Prelude to *Suite No. 6* is the most expansive, a surging *perpetuum mobile* that demands the highest levels of virtuosity. The other movements display their dance origins to a greater or lesser extent: the Gigues, even in the two minor key suites, swing along with enormous energy, whereas the Sarabandes tend to be vehicles for a kind of dignified melancholy, often with much use of double-stopping (a three- or four-note chord broken into two parts).

As the *Suites* progress they become more difficult. In the fifth suite Bach specifies that the A string (the highest) be tuned down a tone to G, thus slightly changing the character of the instrument. The result is the most original and mysterious of all the suites with, at its centre, a Sarabande of the most simple but profound gravity. The final suite has a great deal of high passage work and is the hardest of them all. It was almost certainly written for the violoncello piccolo, an instrument with an added E string at the top – and that's the instrument that is used on our recommended recording.

Pablo Casals was the first modern cellist to rescue the suites from the obscurity into which they had fallen. Since his pioneering recordings in the 1930s, there's been a bewildering number of interpretations which in the last two decades have been supplemented by several which employ a period instrument approach. The "Baroque" sound differs from that of a modern instrument in that it is lighter, leaner and more diffuse. Equally the playing of Anner Bylsma, the doyen of Baroque cellists, tends to stress the delicacy of these pieces rather than their virtuosity. He refuses to dig into the notes, frequently gliding across the strings with the gentlest of touches. Speeds are never extreme, though he does take the Sarabandes at a less leisurely pace than most. His is a spontaneous response to the music that is both flexible and highly imaginative.

Johann Sebastian Bach

Brandenburg Concertos, Nos. 1–6

Il Giardino Armonico; Giovanni Antonini (director)

Teldec 4509-98442-2; 2 CDs; full price

J.S. Bach frequently fell out with his employers, and was even briefly imprisoned by the Duke of Weimar for being too keen to leave his service. When he became Kapellmeister (music director) at the small court of Cöthen in 1717, however, it was for a rather more sympathetic employer, Prince Leopold. A passionate amateur musician, the prince was also a strict Calvinist, which meant that Bach was not called on to compose any religious music but could instead concentrate on orchestral and instrumental music.

Among the many masterpieces that Bach wrote at Cöthen are the six concertos dedicated to the Margrave of Brandenburg but almost certainly written for the Cöthen court orchestra, since their quirky orchestration matches the players known to have been at Bach's disposal. Partly assembled from other compositions, the *Brandenburg Concertos* demonstrate the rich potential of the concerto grosso, a form in which a dynamic interchange between a group of soloists and the full ensemble is the governing principle.

Whereas Handel's concerti grossi (see p.75) are scored entirely for string orchestra and harpsichord, the *Brandenburg Concertos* employ a different set of soloists in each concerto – so instead of a homogeneous texture in which variety is achieved through contrasts of loud and soft, a dialogue is established between different types of sounds. *No. 1* has the oddest solo group (two horns, three oboes, a bassoon and a violin), though *No. 2* is also unusual, calling for recorder, oboe, violin and trumpet. The precedent for this use of a wide variety of instruments was Vivaldi, a composer Bach admired, and the rich colours that emerge from these instrumental mixes are one of the main pleasures of these works.

All the concertos follow the Italian three-movement pattern (fast-slow-fast) with the exception of *No. 1*, which has an extra movement made up of a sequence of dances, and *No. 3*, which has no central movement at all. The fast movements are pushed along by a repeated and rapid pulse known as a motor rhythm. This is another inheritance from Vivaldi, although the interweaving of the individual lines of music – the counterpoint – is far more complex than in the Italian's work. The slow movements, again in imitation of Vivaldi, are often made up of lyrical elongated lines that resemble the opera arias of the time. Bach usually pares down his solo forces here, often alternating the melody between soloists or having one soloist weave exquisite patterns around the voice with the melody.

The most innovative of the six concertos is *No. 5*, which – although employing three soloists – is really dominated by the harpsichord. In the first movement there's a gradual build-up which climaxes in a full-blown cadenza (an extended solo improvisation). The other soloists – violin and the new transverse flute – come into their own in the slow movement but the harpsichord features strongly in the lilting finale, and overall the work seems to point the way to the great keyboard concertos of Mozart.

This 1997 recording shows what an extraordinary variety of different approaches now exist under the general banner of "authenticity". These are exciting and very idiosyncratic performances in which the individual qualities of the soloists come through quite strongly, as if to emphasize the rich colours of Bach's instrumentation – the warm sonority of *Concerto No. 6* (for two violas, two bass viols and a cello), for example, can rarely have sounded so thick and clotted. There is also a sense of these works as display pieces: speeds are lively, accents unpredictable and the more lyrical passages have a greater luxuriance than is usually found in performances of this music.

Johann Sebastian Bach

St Matthew Passion

Anthony Rolfe Johnson, Andreas Schmidt, Barbara Bonney, Ann Monoyios, Anne Sofie von Otter, Michael Chance, Howard Crook, Olaf Bär, Cornelius Hauptmann; London Oratory Junior Choir; Monteverdi Choir; John Eliot Gardiner (conductor)

Archiv 427 648-2; 3 CDs; full price

J.S. Bach spent the last 27 years of his life in Leipzig as Cantor at the Thomasschule (St Thomas School), where his duties were excessively demanding. He taught at the school, provided music for Leipzig's important civic occasions and – most arduously of all – organized the music for St Thomas's and three other churches. For the main Sunday service each week, Bach's major task was to write a new cantata – a setting for singers and instrumentalists of a commentary, written in verse, on the biblical texts used during the service.

Bach's Passion settings, written for Good Friday, are close in style to the cantatas, but with a narrative element. Musical versions of the gospel accounts of Christ's last days had existed since medieval times, but from the mid-seventeenth century additional meditations and commentaries often augmented the storyline. Bach evidently wrote a total of five Passions but only two, those of St John and St Matthew, have survived. In the latter – his greatest choral work – he transforms an already highly emotional genre into a monumental epic, employing a wide variety of musical forms to bring out both the dramatic and the human elements of the story. Indeed, so vivid was his treatment of this most sacred of subjects that some of his congregation regarded the work as inappropriately theatrical and complained to the church authorities.

St Matthew's account of the Passion is found in chapters 26 and 27 of his gospel. In Bach's version, the narration and all direct speech, except that of the chorus, is presented in a declamatory style, derived from opera, called recitative. A tenor sings the part of the Evangelist, a bass the role of Christ, while the remaining "characters" are distributed across a range of voices. Cast as the crowd, the double choir is employed to great effect throughout, getting the most animated and contrapuntal music, which sometimes reaches a level of viciousness that is shockingly direct. Additional texts (by the religious author Picander) supplement the gospel narrative, providing a meditative dimension that takes on a deeply personal quality in the work's many arias. These often combine the solo voice with a prominent solo instrument that weaves an ornately decorative line around the more austere utterance of the vocalist, as in the heart-stopping solo for alto and violin, "Erbarme dich" (Have mercy), which occurs after Peter's denial of Christ.

Though a terrible feeling of tragedy is always present, there is also a strong sense of community that binds all the participants (and the congregation) together. This is partly achieved through the vehicle of the metrical hymns, or chorales, which provide regular oases of calm throughout the drama. This sense of community culminates in the closing chorus, "Wir setzen uns mit Tränen nieder" (In tears of grief, dear Lord, we leave Thee), a deeply moving conclusion that is both funereal and uplifting at the same time.

The *St Matthew Passion* has been staged several times this century, and John Eliot Gardiner's ardently dramatic interpretation immediately makes you realize why. His speeds are faster than most, but always in the service of narrative momentum, as is his use of an extreme dynamic range. The soloists, who seem to have been selected for their clear and open delivery, are uniformly excellent and match the bright and incisive style of the chorus. If this sounds too strident an approach, then rest assured that the more contemplative moments have all the requisite tenderness and sensitivity. All in all this is a remarkable achievement that brings the work alive in the most fresh and vivid fashion.

Samuel Barber

Knoxville: Summer of 1915; Adagio for Strings; Essays Nos. 1 & 2; Overture to The School for Scandal; Medea's Dance of Vengeance

Sylvia McNair (soprano); Atlanta Symphony Orchestra; Yoel Levi (conductor)

Telarc CD-80250; full price

Samuel Barber came from a family steeped in music: his mother was a talented pianist while his aunt, Louise Homer, was an outstanding contralto who sang at the Metropolitan Opera. Barber himself had a fine baritone voice, and even considered a career as a professional singer. Not surprisingly he wrote well and often for the voice, but his orchestral and instrumental works are no less lyrical and melody-centred – a fact that has led him to be unfairly dismissed by some critics as a lightweight sentimentalist. It's an unfair description: in his best work, Barber combines a romantic sensibility with a rigorous and, essentially classical, economy of means that is powerfully and directly communicative.

Barber's name has become synonymous with one composition above all others: the undeniably beautiful *Adagio for Strings*, which began life as the slow movement of his 1936 *String Quartet*. Two years later Barber arranged it for string orchestra and, with the help of Toscanini, it lodged itself indelibly in the American psyche. With its slow-building melodic lines, breath-like pauses, and general mood of subdued sadness it is not difficult to see why it has taken on the status of a twentieth-century classic. It was broadcast at the death of President Roosevelt and more recently provided emotional catharsis in Oliver Stone's Vietnam film *Platoon*.

In 1946 Barber received a commission to write a ballet for the dancer and choreographer Martha Graham. The two of them settled on the *Medea* myth but decided to treat it in a way that would emphasize the theme of jealous destructive love. Barber provided a score which was uncharacteristically terse and edgy, with piano and percussion used to create an atmosphere of mounting tension. The ballet climaxes in the frenetic *Dance of Vengeance*, in which Graham gradually pulled out an extended red ribbon from within her costume, symbolizing the biliousness and corrosive power of her rage.

A year later, when the soprano Eleanor Steber asked Barber for a new work to perform with the Boston Symphony Orchestra, the composer turned to the writings of James Agee, which he had recently been reading. The result was one of his finest works, *Knoxville: Summer of 1915*, an unashamedly nostalgic evocation of a child's view of small-town family life, as American as Thornton Wilder's *Our Town* or Aaron Copland's near-contemporary *Appalachian Spring* (see p.49). Barber set Agee's prose poem – a mix of the simple and the overly poetic – in a largely syllabic and straightforward manner which stays close to the rhythms and inflexions of the original. Musically it is dominated by a gentle undulating melody which frames the piece and suggests both a lullaby and the movement of a rocking chair on a porch. A more animated middle section (representing the clatter of the streetcar) leads into a brief rhapsodic passage as night falls. Barber's restraint and real identification with the material avoids sentimentality and creates a genuinely moving picture.

Knoxville is a marvellous vehicle for a lyric soprano (preferably an American one) but it's not an easy work to bring off. Sylvia McNair has a beautiful full and rounded voice and does as well as anyone at expressing the easy-going, every-day innocence of the work, especially in the opening passages. It comes with a broodingly atmospheric account of the *Adagio*, in which conductor Levi judges the work's dark ebb and flow to perfection and resists the temptation to overdo the pathos. The disc also includes a selection of Barber's better-known orchestral works, including the two concentrated *Orchestral Essays* and the early *Overture to The School for Scandal*.

Béla Bartók

String Quartets Nos. 1–6

Takács Quartet

Decca 455 297-2; 2 CDs; full price

Bartók's six string quartets, written between 1908 and 1939, plot the entire trajectory of his development, from the Debussy-esque atmospherics of the first and second, through the harshness of the third and fourth, to the more direct communication of the last pair. Bartók was not a string player and this perhaps liberated his imagination into seeking out new and often abrasive sonorities. Certainly these are extremely free-ranging and original works, full of weird sounds and fluctuating rhythms. String quartets tend to be like conversations between four voices, but in Bartók's there are times when the protagonists seem to be speaking different languages.

Of the six the last three are the most rewarding, with *No. 4* justly celebrated for its magical slow movement. This begins with a rhapsodic cello line but at its heart is a quivering evocation of the nocturnal sounds of nature – fluttering wings, the chirruping and twittering of insects – all woven together into a single mysterious moment. This quartet has a symmetrical pattern, with the slow movement framed by two Scherzos, the first played with muted strings, the second employing a typically Bartókian instruction that the strings be plucked so hard that they twang against the finger-board. The finale transforms some of the ideas of the first movement into a frenzied, whirling dance.

Quartet No. 5 is another symmetrical five-movement work. A hard-driven and aggressive theme in octaves begins the opening

Allegro and sets the mood for the whole movement. With the Adagio a delicate, sombre chorale-like theme in the lower strings suddenly gives way to more hallucinatory sounds touched with sadness. The central Scherzo is a restless dance in characteristically broken-up rhythmic chunks; the penultimate movement has connections with the earlier slow movement but with a greater air of anxiety, while the finale is dominated by a wild improvisatory quality that reaches frenetic levels of activity before breaking off to deliver an incongruous fragment of a banal dance tune.

The last work Bartók wrote in Europe, the *Quartet No. 6* is the most introspective of his quartets. Two psychological blows struck him as he wrote it – the start of World War II and the death of his mother. In some sense the quartet is a threnody for the life that he was to abandon when he emigrated to America. Each of its four movements begins with a slow, mournful opening: a long wistful viola solo states the work's main theme, which is repeated by a sombre cello over restless tremolos in the second movement, then in meandering polyphonic form in the remaining two. The second halves of the first three movements are contrastingly harsh, reaching a level of bitterness and sarcasm in the middle movements. The music reaches a grotesque level in the third-movement Scherzo, in which a slashing dance full of folkish off-beats lurches its way along, briefly interrupted by a lyrical pastoral interlude. The finale is pure despair, the main theme's treatment becoming more and more directionless and etiolated until it finally disintegrates into silence.

There are several recordings of the Bartók quartets that have more polish than these performances, but few with such a level of commitment, flair and excitement. The Takács Quartet don't just play the notes: they seem to inhabit completely Bartók's extraordinary sound-world. The rhythmic contortions, the unexpected changes of mood, the lurking folk elements – all are perfectly judged and handled with complete assurance. *Quartet No. 6*, in particular, gets a beautiful reading, the pain, frustration and despair gradually becoming more explicit as each movement unfolds.

Béla Bartók

Concerto for Orchestra; Music for Strings, Percussion and Celesta

Oslo Philharmonic Orchestra; Mariss Jansons (conductor)

EMI CDC7 54070 2; full price

Between 1905 and 1918 the Hungarian composer Béla Bartók recorded and annotated thousands of Eastern European folk songs and dances. As well as comprising an invaluable ethno-musicological record of a vanishing world, Bartók's researches constantly fed into his own compositions. Nearly all the music of his maturity reveals the influence, direct or indirect, of mainly Hungarian, Transylvanian and Slovakian folk music. It is discernible in the variety of scale forms he employed, in the rhythms and textures he favoured, and in his reluctance ever to repeat a phrase or motif in exactly the same way.

Bartók's most strikingly original orchestral work is the *Music for Strings, Percussion and Celesta* of 1936. Written in four contrasting movements, the work begins with muted strings playing an unusually sombre and uneasy-sounding fugue that builds quietly and obsessively to a climactic cymbal clash from which it then descends. The Allegro that follows is a highly energetic dance movement in which a dynamic interchange of ideas and material takes place between two string groups placed on opposite sides of the stage. But it's the unnervingly eerie Adagio which makes the greatest impact. The opening tapping of a single note on the xylophone, the ethereal high strings, the steady "tread" of the piano – all these disparate sounds create a nightmare world that is chilly and inhuman (a characteristic that Stanley Kubrick cleverly exploited when using it in the soundtrack of *The Shining*). This mood is abruptly dissipated by the finale, a scurrying collection of wild folk dances, one following hard upon the other, that culminates with a return of the fugue theme and a new harmonic richness.

Five years later Bartók fled war-torn Hungary for the US, where he struggled to make ends meet. He'd almost stopped composing when he received a commission from Serge Koussevitsky, principal conductor of the Boston Symphony Orchestra. The result was the five-movement *Concerto for Orchestra*, a deliberately accessible symphonic work that displays Bartók's gift for deft orchestral colouring and his predilection for symmetrical structures. At its centre is the deeply mysterious Elegia, a "lugubrious death-song", according to Bartók, whose atmospheric sonorities produce a mood of anguish close in spirit to his early opera *Bluebeard's Castle*. The movements on each side of the Elegia are light and witty. The mischievous second movement – a "game of couples" – has pairs of wind instruments playing in fixed intervals (flutes in fifths, oboes in thirds etc) with at its centre a serene chorale played by the brass. The fourth movement has two extremely fresh, folk-inflected themes that are rudely interrupted by the march theme from Shostakovich's seventh symphony, which Bartók loathed and which is mocked by the ensuing orchestral response. The first and last movements are both swirling rushes of unbridled energy, but whereas the first is rather serious in tone the last has an exuberance and an assertiveness which is surely intended as a tribute to New World confidence.

There are several very good historical accounts of these works, but this 1990 recording combines outstanding performances with the kind of bright modern sound that really benefits the clean textures of Bartók's orchestral music. In particular the *Music for Strings, Percussion and Celesta* has a clarity of detail that really brings home the strangeness of the instrumental timbres, with the Adagio sounding particularly spooky. Jansons' account of the *Concerto for Orchestra* is invigoratingly dynamic. This is a virtuoso work that allows an orchestra no weaknesses, and the Oslo Philharmonic meets the challenges head on, nowhere more excitingly than in the sparking finale, which it carries off with finesse and panache.

Ludwig van Beethoven

Piano Sonatas No. 8 ("Pathétique"), No. 23 ("Appassionata") and No. 31

Emil Gilels

Deutsche Grammophon 439 426-2; mid-price

Like Mozart, with whom he briefly studied, Beethoven was a brilliant pianist, admired, in particular, for the passion of his playing and for his amazing powers of improvisation – whether it be on a given theme or in developing an idea within a sonata movement. Nearly all his piano compositions were written with himself in mind as their performer, but these sonatas did more than extend the technical range of what was thought possible on the instrument – they opened up new depths of feeling.

The *Pathétique*, his most important early sonata, was written in 1798–99. It's in C minor, a key well suited to the expression of pathos, hence Beethoven's own title for it – *Grand sonata pathétique*. Showing signs of his dissatisfaction with classical form, this is a grandiose but at times desperate work, reflecting Beethoven's awareness of the deterioration in his hearing. It begins unusually with a slow, portentous introduction that acts as a kind of prelude to the tempestuous drama of the ensuing Allegro. The solemn central movement achieves a poignant sense of resignation, largely through its sheer simplicity – an achingly lyrical melody is set against a steady and almost prosaic background accompaniment. The finale is a quicksilver Rondo that exudes a neurotic restlessness.

In Beethoven's own opinion, his greatest sonata was the *Sonata No. 23* (1804), a titanic four-movement work of extreme emotional and technical challenges. The initial Allegro, with its ghostly echo of the fifth symphony's opening theme, exerts an ominous power while the succeeding Andante takes a rather quirky slow march and develops into a set of highly original variations – full of odd, off-the-beat emphases. But it is the last movement that justifies the nickname *Appassionata*. This shattering finale is introduced by a series of crashing, repeated chords followed by a torrential burst of semiquavers that supports the defiant main theme. A number of pauses, introduced by rapid and aggressive octave passages, precedes the coda – one minute of uninterrupted mayhem.

With his last five sonatas, Beethoven took keyboard writing into a new domain, in which the standard forms of classical music were invested with a profound emotional potency. Of these, the penultimate sonata is one of the most magical, if least known. Much of it sounds superficially conventional, the opening distinctly Mozartian in its singing right-hand tune above strumming chords, the magnificent finale alternating a deeply introspective theme with a gentle and elusive Bach-like fugue. What makes it so original is the way Beethoven steers the music towards completely unexpected destinations, especially in terms of the harmony, which seems to feel its way into an utterly fresh musical world. Even now the visionary aspect of this music sounds startling, and it was a direction that none of Beethoven's successors felt able to follow.

One of the tragedies of recording history is that the Ukrainian pianist Emil Gilels died just five short of completing a full set of Beethoven sonatas. This disc compellingly illustrates why he was so revered as a Beethoven interpreter. As with so many Russian-trained pianists, Gilels is technically irreproachable: he possesses a rich and varied tone but he uses it in a much more extreme way than does, for example, Wilhelm Kempff (see p.22). His playing tends to emphasize contrasts – of tone, of dynamics and of speed – while retaining a firm sense of the music's overall structure. Both the *Pathétique* and *Appassionata* pulsate with a nervous, flashing vibrancy that is always convincing, never histrionic. But it is in the ruminative finale of *Sonata No. 31* that the subtlety of detail in his playing really comes to the fore.

Ludwig van Beethoven

String Quartet No. 13 in B flat (Op. 130); Grosse Fuge (Op. 133)

Lindsay String Quartet

ASV CD DCA 603; full price

Beethoven began his last five string quartets in 1822, after a gap of twelve years, prompted by one Prince Galitzin, an amateur cellist, who commissioned the first three of the sequence. As spare and intense as the last five piano sonatas, these astonishing compositions are marked by an increasing predilection for a polyphonic style, evident not only in movements that are overtly fugal but also in episodes where the four separate parts create a sense of four minds combining for the perfect expression of a single idea.

Beethoven was competely deaf when he wrote these quartets, and a sense of the composer thinking out loud, with the listener as a kind of privileged eavesdropper, pervades much of the music. Not surprisingly, neither the first players nor the audience could come to terms with works of such originality. Even today the dramatic changes of speed and unexpected harmonies sound startling, though this music is not as relentlessly serious as some have suggested. What makes it ultimately so satisfying is precisely the demands that it makes: here is music which, unlike some, calls for an active and concentrated listening response before it will yield up its magic.

Each of the five quartets is a masterpiece but two of them, *Quartets Nos. 13* and *14*, reach levels of profundity astonishing even for Beethoven. *Quartet No. 13* is the most contentious since its last movement took the form of a colossal fugue, the *Grosse Fuge* (Great Fugue), which was found to be too difficult by the original performers. Beethoven later substituted a safe alternative finale that bore little relation to the remainder of the work. The preceding five movements are beautifully poised between complexity and an absolute directness of utterance. Movements alternate between slow and fast, beginning with a brooding, autumnal Adagio which is punctuated by sudden flurries of rapid counterpoint. There's an easy-going charm to the three central movements, which precede the heart of the work, the Cavatina. There is a floating, suspended quality to this extraordinary musical episode which seems to reveal an unparalleled degree of despair.

The *Grosse Fuge* is today played both as the quartet's finale and as an independent work. It's easy to see why it originally caused so much alarm. Running to 745 bars and lasting nearly twenty minutes, it's a work of the most dramatic extremes, hardly warranting the description of chamber music. Its first section is dominated by an incessant rocking rhythm that creates the near-unbearable sense of anguish that is the fugue's salient characteristic. There are brief oases of calm but the overall effect is of an anger-driven dynamism bordering on the edge of incoherence.

In this recording the Lindsay Quartet perform the *Quartet No. 13* as originally written, with the alternative finale tagged on as an appendix. Of all the recent interpreters of the late quartets, the Lindsays are the ones that like to live most dangerously. Their playing is uninhibited, forceful and direct, and they treat the music as if it were the spiritual autobiography of Beethoven's last years. Speeds and dynamics are often pushed to extremes as if to maximize the inner drama of the music and there is a wonderful spontaneity to the playing. Occasionally this passion comes at the expense of ensemble and intonation (the *Grosse Fuge*, at moments, sounds strident and demented). More often it is thrillingly successful: the Cavatina can rarely have sounded so heart-wrenchingly beautiful, and throughout there is that electric sense of occasion usually found only in the concert hall.

Ludwig van Beethoven /
Felix Mendelssohn

Violin Concertos

Yehudi Menuhin (violin); Philharmonia Orchestra; Berlin Philharmonic;
Wilhelm Furtwängler (conductor)

EMI CDM 5 66875 2; mid-price

Uniquely among the great violin concertos, Beethoven's avoids any real virtuosic display. Perhaps that's why, at the premiere in 1806, the original soloist, Franz Clement, felt obliged to insert his own sonata between the first and second movements, playing it on one string on a violin held upside down. After this inauspicious start the concerto remained lost in obscurity for several decades until the violinist Joseph Joachim rescued it and gave a series of memorable performances, conducted by Felix Mendelssohn.

The concerto's opening is beautifully simple: four crotchets, tapped out on the kettledrum, followed by a simple hymn like melody in the woodwind that establishes a mood of supreme tranquillity, which is maintained throughout the long first movement. The orchestral introduction lasts about three minutes, at which point the violin appears, as if from nowhere, in a serene rising phrase like a bird taking flight. All the thematic material stated by the orchestra is repeated and embellished by the violin. The slow movement Larghetto is even more ethereal: again the principal theme is simple and dignified, featuring brief silences which, in the theme's second statement, are filled with exquisite decorative sallies from the soloist. The exquisite tenderness of this movement is rudely shattered by the earthy boisterousness of the finale, a Rondo in which the soloist finally gets to show off a bit.

Whereas Beethoven's concerto achieves eloquence through understatement, Mendelssohn's *Violin Concerto in E minor* wears its heart on its sleeve. Written in 1844, it's a late work and one that firmly rebuts the idea that the precocious composer lost most of his inspiration after the age of 20. Dispensing with any orchestral introduction, the soloist pitches straight in with a passionately surging melody that verges on the melodramatic. In contrast the movement's second subject is quiet and confiding, a moment of intimacy before the restlessness of the first theme returns. Even more moving is the song-like simplicity of the Andante, a movement that has been accused of sentimentality but which has all the lucid directness of a great Mozart aria. With the finale, Mendelssohn returns to the energetic lightness of his *A Midsummer Night's Dream Overture*. Where Beethoven's last movement was a rustic sing-song, Mendelssohn's is an elusive dance with the violin's playful scamperings frequently shadowed by a woodwind instrument as if in hot pursuit. It's a suitably high-spirited ending to what is the most straightforwardly enjoyable of all nineteenth-century concertos.

Yehudi Mehuhin began studying the Beethoven concerto when he was just eight, and this recording, made in 1953, reveals him at the height of his powers: the tone is sweet but never simpering, the sense of line assured and firm. His partnership with Wilhelm Furtwängler was brave, since, as a Jew, Menuhin was expected to steer clear of musicians who had remained in Nazi Germany during the war. Instead he felt the conductor's motives for remaining (to preserve the real spirit of German culture in the face of Nazi barbarism) were honourable, and he saw their collaboration as a means of healing old wounds. Both men regarded music as a spiritual force and their rapport is abundantly clear in this performance which seems, paradoxically, both spontaneous and inevitable. The Mendelssohn, recorded a year earlier, is another classic. Menuhin employs a marginally more gutsy tone to his playing but the same sense of the music's unstoppable flow is no less apparent. The recording quality, though nearly fifty years old, is exceptional.

Ludwig van Beethoven

Piano Concertos Nos. 4 and 5

Wilhelm Kempff (piano); Berlin Philharmonic Orchestra; Ferdinand Leitner (conductor)

Deutsche Grammophon DG 447 402 2; mid-price

Beethoven's five piano concertos overthrew the formula of the eighteenth century. Until the emergence of Beethoven, every movement of a concerto began with the piano repeating or developing an opening theme played by the orchestra, sometimes taking over the material on its own but never battling openly with the "accompaniment". Beethoven, recognizing the concerto's potential for dramatic conflict, gave the protagonists material to be played independently of each other while working towards a common goal. He was helped by advances in piano manufacture which, during his life, extended the instrument's range to six and a half octaves. Even so, in his last two concertos, there's a real sense of Beethoven straining against the limitations of the instruments at his disposal.

Piano Concerto No. 4, the last of Beethoven's piano concertos to be performed by him, was completed in 1807. It begins unusually, with the piano alone stating a gently rocking opening theme which the orchestra then takes up, leaving the piano silent. A sense of mystery has been established and when the soloist eventually reappears it's with an almost improvisatory flourish. It's a long and expansive movement, essentially sunny in mood but with a definite undertow of melancholy, in which the soloist ranges widely, from the rapturous to the introspective. The short Andante takes the form of a dialogue between fierce, pithy statements from the orchestra and reticient – almost timid – reponses from the piano which suddenly blossom into a cadenza-like passage of great poignancy. The Rondo finale is extremely dramatic: a predominantly feverish abandon is interrupted by a wistful second subject on the piano which is exquisitely echoed by the woodwind.

With his last and greatest piano concerto, written in 1809, Beethoven forces the genre into the most heroic of forms (though its nickname, the *Emperor*, was not of his choosing). The piano now really stands up to the orchestra which, at the outset, does little more than announce the soloist's entry with a few chords. The piano then lets loose a flood of sound that washes over the orchestra before attacking a cadenza of great difficulty which, eventually, allows the orchestra back in to pursue a long exposition of all the movement's main themes. The piano is first among equals here, though in Beethoven's day it would have had a real struggle asserting itself. No such problem occurs in the spiritually charged delicacy of the Adagio, where after a sombre but deeply felt orchestral introduction (whose ending is tantalizingly delayed) the piano enters high up with the simplest of descending melodies against a minimal accompaniment. It's the most extraordinarily touching moment, the crystalline purity of the piano's tone conveying both confidence and frailty. A bridge passage of lightly touched chords leads into the last movement, as spirited a Rondo as Beethoven wrote but with an extra symphonic dimension to it.

Wilhelm Kempff was one of this century's most refined and poetic Beethoven players. Not for him the overblown gestures that some pianists resort to in these concertos – instead his playing is constantly alive to the more mercurial aspects of these works, their capacity (especially in the long first movement) to express myriad emotions. Kempff's Beethoven is at heart an improviser, a fantasist and a proto-Romantic, and this view of the music is communicated through a wide range of tonal colouring and in a manner that is strong without being over-assertive. Both slow movements are miracles of eloquent understatement but in the *Emperor* Kempff achieves a translucent clarity which, with Leitner's beautifully phrased accompaniment, is especially affecting.

Ludwig van Beethoven

Symphonies Nos. 5 and 7

Vienna Philharmonic Orchestra; Carlos Kleiber (conductor)

Deutsche Grammophon DG 447 400-2; mid-price

Beethoven was a student of Haydn and a great admirer of Mozart, and his first two symphonies were written with their examples before him. But with his *Symphony No. 3*, he shook off all influences and initiated a sea-change as profound as any in the history of music. Beethoven did not so much alter the form of the symphony as expand its possibilities: instrumentation became richer, a conscious attempt was made to link movements, and the development of thematic material became more elaborate. This was orchestral music on the grandest possible scale, containing the very foundations of Romanticism in its grandiose gestures and defiant individualism. Nowhere is this more thrillingly realized than in the restless subjectivity of the *Symphony No. 5*.

The electrifying theme that opens the symphony is, surely, the most famous four notes in music. It dominates the first movement, even nagging away in the cellos and basses when the lyrical second theme appears. The idea that it represents "fate knocking at the door" is a fanciful one, but undoubtedly its stark directness has a thrilling urgency that sets the tone for much of the symphony, in which only the second movement Andante – variations on two expansive themes – imparts any real sense of calm. An uneasy tension pervades the Scherzo (Beethoven's more manic alternative to the usual Minuet), a movement that swings between mystery and stridency, until a moment of magical suspension leads into the triumphant blaze of the finale. The latter is as gloriously affirmative a movement as Beethoven ever wrote, the additional three trombones and double bassoon adding a marvellous breadth to the sound. E.T.A. Hoffmann, the only contemporary critic to understand the work, thought the finale's opening had the impact of "radiant, blinding sunlight which suddenly illuminates the dark night".

If the *Symphony No. 5* plots a course from darkness to light, then *Symphony No. 7*, written four years later in 1812, is – with the exception of its sombre slow movement – a far more consistently exuberant affair. Dubbed by Wagner "the apotheosis of the dance", it opens with a slow and grandiose introduction leading to an energetic Vivace, in which Beethoven juxtaposes rhythms derived from Sicilian dance music with a cleverly syncopated melody. In contrast, the ensuing Allegretto is dark and subdued, its austere main theme a simple funeral march whose subsequent variations build to an increasingly fervent level. The remaining movements return to the inspiration of dance: a mischievous Scherzo gives way to a Trio that grows more and more solemn until the Scherzo is reprised. The final Allegro is a frenetic whirligig of unbridled energy in which a foot-stamping tune of two beats in the bar (the accent on the second beat) alternates with a more refined and balletic second theme. It's as if Beethoven were pushing the Viennese obsession for dance music to ever more exhausting extremes.

Carlos Kleiber is a conductor who makes few recordings, but when he does go into the studio he invariably has something new and exciting to say about a work. These two Beethoven recordings, made in the mid-1970s, are marked by a radically dynamic and non-reverential approach to the music. Speeds are often brisk, and there's a tautness to the conducting that keeps the tension running high but never out of control. *Symphony No.5* has an almost driven quality to it that actually adds to the work's sense of gravity and power. It's also notable that in the slower movements of both symphonies Kleiber refuses to wallow, instead allowing the music to unfold with a steady organic flow.

Ludwig van Beethoven

Symphony No. 9

Elisabeth Schwarzkopf, Elisabeth Höngen, Hans Hopf, Otto Edelmann; Choir and Orchestra of the Bayreuth Festival; Wilhelm Furtwängler (conductor)

EMI CDM 5 66901 2; mid-price

Most of the music of Beethoven's last years is profoundly inward-looking and anguished. The obvious exception is the *Symphony No. 9*, a work which envisions a Utopian future of universal brotherhood and is addressed to the whole of humanity. Hence the tendency to play it at highly charged historical occasions that call for a tone of heroic optimism: the fall of the Berlin Wall in 1989, for instance or, as in this recording, the re-opening of the Bayreuth Festival in a Germany still badly damaged by war.

Beethoven's most striking innovation in the ninth symphony was to employ a chorus and four soloists in the finale. He first had the idea of setting Schiller's *Ode to Joy* in 1792, but it was not until 1823–24 that he decided to incorporate it into a symphony. Further ensuring the consternation of the conservative Viennese, Beethoven made the last movement the emotional climax of the work: symphonies previously were conceived in terms of contrast between succeeding episodes, with the last movement invariably fast and light. In *Symphony No. 9* everything leads to the finale.

The opening bars are tense and mysterious, building gradually to a declamation of the main theme. This is a movement of epic dimensions, its rugged implacability barely modified by the more lyrical second subject. Beethoven breaks with his own custom by having the Scherzo as the second movement, a hard-driven quasi-dance that seems on the brink of disintegrating under its own head of steam. Nothing in these two movements prepares one for the deep solemnity of the long Adagio, a creation that's almost unbearably moving in its troubled tranquillity.

The finale's clamorous introduction leads to a review of all the symphony's previous themes before rejecting them in favour of the *Ode to Joy* theme, an amazingly simple melody which employs a mere five notes. Beethoven introduces it gently at first, then allows it to grow in boldness. A repetition of the opening is halted by the poem's opening lines, delivered like a clarion by the bass soloist: "O friends, not these tones, but let us rather sing more pleasant and joyful ones". The chorus and other soloists respond to the call. The melody then transforms into a jaunty march led by the tenor and is followed by a long orchestral interlude which leads to the core of the movement – a religiose invocation to universal fraternity that suddenly explodes into a rapturous statement of joy. After a short meditative section by the soloists, the symphony ends with a final euphoric rush of energy.

This live recording was made at the Bayreuth Festspielhaus in 1951. Furtwängler initially didn't want the concert recorded and problems of balance have not been entirely solved by the engineers. There are also moments – most disturbingly some tentative horn playing in the middle of the Adagio – when the actual performance seems on the verge of collapse. And yet unquestionably this is one of the most overwhelming accounts of any symphony ever recorded. Furtwängler was a highly subjective interpreter who never gave two identical performances of any work. In this performance, the whole piece moves along with all the power and unpredictability of a great river. At its centre is a heart-rending account of the Adagio (sounding amazingly close to Mahler), immensely slow and with the most beautiful string sound. The finale, by comparison, is startlingly vibrant, full of dramatic pauses and sudden changes of speed. It generates an excitement and a sense of occasion that remains unrivalled.

Alban Berg

Violin Concerto

Anne-Sophie Mutter (violin); Chicago Symphony Orchestra; James Levine (conductor)

Deutsche Grammophon 437 093-2; with Wolfgang Rihm, *Gesungene Zeit*; full price

Schoenberg's two most talented pupils, Alban Berg and Anton Webern, were also his closest followers. Both embraced the twelve-tone system of composition formulated by Schoenberg in the early 1920s (see p.144), but Berg did so with a greater freedom, often creating tone rows that resulted in rich, tonal-sounding harmony. He was by nature a Romantic, and the emotional impact that his music made was always of great importance to him.

Of all Berg's compositions, the most touchingly direct is the *Violin Concerto*, written in 1935. It was commissioned by the Russian–American violinist Louis Krasner, but its composition was prompted by the death of Manon Gropius, the 18-year-old daughter of Alma Mahler (to whom Berg was close) and the architect Walter Gropius. Berg broke off from working on his opera *Lulu* and wrote the concerto in about three months, inscribing the finished copy with the words "to the memory of an angel". Four months later, as a result of blood poisoning, Berg himself was dead, leaving *Lulu* uncompleted.

Berg's *Violin Concerto* is an attempt, in the composer's own words, "to translate characteristics of the young girl's nature into musical terms." It is in two movements, with the most magical opening of any modern concerto: the violin emerges playing on open strings – it is tuned in fifths – against an orchestral background also in fifths.

It's a gentle beginning, subdued and melancholy, from which the tone row (the fixed ordering of the twelve notes of the chromatic scale that underpins the work) gradually appears. Berg's tone row is such that it enables him to make allusions to tonal harmony throughout the work. As the first movement becomes more agitated, he quotes a Carinthian folk tune – a secret reference to his youthful relationship with a woman who bore his illegitimate daughter. Berg enjoyed introducing such coded messages into his music but greater significance lies in the way he creates a sense of suspension by sustaining a tension between the work's tonal-melodic aspect and its atonal-abstract one.

The second movement, Allegro-Adagio, is initially more violent, the violin roaming restlessly like a troubled spirit within a harsh landscape of snarling brass and rumbling timpani. There's an extended cadenza-like passage that is more subdued in tone but the overall dark mood suggests death as something agonizing and catastrophic. Then suddenly everything changes and, as if from another world, Berg quietly introduces the melody of the Lutheran chorale *Es ist genug* ("It is enough; Lord, if it pleases you set me free"). It's a spine-tingling moment and the intensity is sustained to the movement's end as the chorale is subjected to a series of numinous transformations – at one point it is intoned by the woodwind in Bach's harmonization as the violin whispers anxiously around it. The ending is haunting and unresolved – the violin climbs uneasily to a sustained high note as the opening sequence of fifths ripples softly underneath it.

Even without knowing of the circumstances under which it was written, Berg's *Violin Concerto* seems to represent a struggle between life and death or, perhaps more accurately, the memory of a life and the acceptance of loss. Anne-Sophie Mutter is particularly sensitive to the work's ambivalence, and her performance is rich in detail, with a firm-centred tone which is warm without ever being sentimental. Her playing inspired the other piece on the disc, Wolfgang Rihm's *Gesungene Zeit* (Time Chant). This is an intensely focused work for violin and orchestra, much of it written for the higher reaches of the violin's register, that achieves a timeless meditative stasis.

Hector Berlioz / Benjamin Britten

Les Nuits d'été] Les Illuminations

Barbara Hendricks (soprano); English Chamber Orchestra; Colin Davis (conductor)

EMI CDC5 55053 2; full price

Berlioz was famous, not to say infamous, for doing things on the grandest possible scale, but he was also a master of small-scale composition, and his numerous songs are testament to his refined melodic gift. The greatest of these songs are *Les Nuits d'été* (Summer Nights), a setting of six poems by Berlioz's friend and fellow journalist Théophile Gautier. Berlioz published them in 1841 in an edition for mezzo-soprano (or tenor) and piano, but later orchestrated *Les Nuits d'été*, making it the first ever orchestral song cycle.

Gautier's poems are mostly concerned with love, but usually within a context of death or separation. Berlioz's selection frames four rather morbid poems with two lighthearted ones. The first, *Villanelle*, describes two lovers venturing out of doors at the first sign of spring. It's a simple, radiant melody, with a light strumming accompaniment in which, from the second verse onward, fragments of the melody are echoed in the orchestra. When he orchestrated the second song, *La spectre de la rose*, Berlioz added a long brooding introduction, and throughout the piece the orchestral writing dramatizes the soprano's flowing line in a way that elevates Gautier's tale of the lingering presence of a cut flower to something genuinely tragic. The next three songs reinforce the mood of longing for something lost. In *Sur les lagunes* a man mourns the death of his lover against music that suggests the movement of a boat on the water, each verse ending with a heartfelt and desperate cry. *Absence* is less bleak but no less sad, while in *Au cimitière* (In the cemetery) the simple chordal accompaniment sets the plaintive quality of the vocal line in stark relief. The atmosphere changes with the final song *L'ile inconnu* (The unknown isle) into something ecstatic – the poet asks his love which exotic place she would like to visit and she replies: a land "where love endures for ever".

Nearly a hundred years later, the English composer Benjamin Britten turned to the French language in order to liberate himself from the rather constricting (and often precious) world of English song. *Les Illuminations* (1939) is a setting of eight obliquely erotic and elusive verses by Arthur Rimbaud for soprano and string orchestra. The cycle evokes a hallucinatory world in which images of the modern city and a luxurious depiction of the god Pan exist side by side. There is also a tightness and economy to the music that reflects Britten's awareness of contemporaries like Stravinsky and Poulenc. He creates some glorious effects, and there is often an harmonic disjunction within songs which increases the poetry's sense of ambiguity. The line that frames the cycle, "J'ai seul la clef de cette parade sauvage" (I alone hold the key to this savage parade) suggests that this piece had a special significance to Britten: it is certainly one of his most vivid and inspired shorter works.

Berlioz dedicated each of the six songs of *Les Nuits d'été* to different singers, but these days it's nearly always sung by just one – usually a soprano. There are only a few satisfying recordings around, perhaps because it needs a dramatic singer who is capable of subtlety, elegance and restraint. Barbara Hendricks is close to ideal: the voice is occasionally a little hard in the upper register, but she has a lightness of touch – especially in the first and last songs – that is refreshing, and in the more melancholy songs conveys a real sensitivity to the meaning of the words. If anything her voice is even better suited to the Britten, which receives a marvellously sparkling performance.

Hector Berlioz

Symphonie fantastique; Hungarian March; Trojan March; The Corsair and Roman Carnival overtures

Detroit Symphony Orchestra; Paul Paray (conductor)

Mercury 434 328-2; mid-price

Six years after Beethoven's *Symphony No. 9*, the young French composer Hector Berlioz wrote a fifty-minute orchestral work that turned the conventions of the symphony upside down. Subtitled "Episodes in the Life of an Artist", the *Symphonie fantastique* is the feverish expression of the composer's own tortured psyche, a phantasmagoria of changing moods and scenes that paved the way for an intensely subjective strain within nineteenth-century music. Born out of his infatuation with a young Irish actress called Harriet Smithson (whom he had first seen as Ophelia), the symphony is divided into five movements, for which Berlioz provided a written "programme" or key. Descriptive music had certainly existed before (Vivaldi's *Four Seasons* is the obvious example), but no composer had attempted to present so specific a narrative outside of a theatrical context.

Berlioz's principal innovation in the symphony is the use of a theme – an *idée fixe* he called it – that recurs throughout the work. Representing his beloved Harriet, the theme's initially demure appearance in the first movement ("Reveries – Passions") takes on an increasingly fervent character, reaching an almost sexual level of intensity by the movement's end. Throughout the symphony there's a sense that uncontrollable emotion is never far away, as periods of calm are suddenly shattered by music suggesting grief or jealous rage. The second movement evokes a ballroom full of waltzing couples, the "Harriet" theme flitting ominously across it; the long third movement, an Adagio, suggests a pastoral landscape (oboe and cor anglais simulate shepherds calling to each other across the hills) into which the *idée fixe* is introduced with great pathos by high strings. This movement, perhaps more than any other, illustrates Berlioz's genius as an orchestrator: his choice and combination of instruments is always precise, economical and unfailingly vivid – one beautiful moment has the kettledrums and cor anglais suggesting the sound of distant thunder.

With the final two movements we enter the realms of nightmare and misogynistic self-pity. In the most famous movement, "March to the Scaffold", the artist imagines his own execution for the murder of his beloved – the *idée fixe* is conpicuously absent from this section. It's a powerful and relentless episode which, once again, makes its impact not merely through a memorably taut melody but in the way that melody is transformed through brilliant orchestral colouring and an increasing urgency. The movement ends with a loud chord representing the drop of the guillotine blade and the thump of the head in the basket. In the finale, "Dream of a Witches' Sabbath", a grotesquely distorted version of the *idée fixe* represents the mocking presence of the murdered woman at a gathering of demons and monsters. The theme is interrupted by ringing bells and a rasping account of the plainsong Dies irae on low brass, before both melodies battle it out with a mounting air of hysteria and finality.

Several outstanding recordings have been made of Berlioz's masterpiece and this one rates among the very best. Paul Paray's relationship with the Detroit Symphony Orchestra was at its height when this recording was made in 1959, and there's a freshness and an incisiveness to the playing which is spellbinding. Paray was not the kind of conductor to resort to melodrama, but this is a tremendously exciting performance: brooding, darkly imaginative and with a ferocious energy which borders on the demented, above all in the final movement. The Mercury label was at the forefront of hi-fi experimentation in the '50s, and this recording, made on just three microphones, is astonishingly clear and natural sounding.

Pierre Boulez

Rituel in memoriam Bruno Maderna; Éclat/Multiples

BBC Symphony Orchestra; Ensemble InterContemporain; Pierre Boulez (conductor)

Sony SMK 45839; full price

As both conductor and composer, Pierre Boulez has proselytized with remorseless zeal on behalf of the avant-garde for over half a century. For this he has won respect but also a degree of enmity. For all those who regard his work as an inspiringly radical re-appraisal of the fundamentals of music, there are as many who find his pro-modernist polemics tedious and his compositions arid. In fact, although in his early work he could be aggressively dissonant, much of his small output can be fitted into a tradition of French music which includes Debussy and Messiaen, a tradition primarily concerned with the creation of rich and exotic sonorities.

Much of Boulez's music has a pulse-less, static quality, which forces concentration onto the specific and varied sounds that individual instruments are capable of producing. In *Éclat*, the title of which connotes the sight and sound of something dynamic and luminous, Boulez sets up two groups of instruments of different sound types: a nine-piece percussion group (including keyboards and plucked stringed instruments) and a six-piece group comprising strings, brass and wind instruments. *Éclat* explores the differences between them, between sounds that die away soon after being made and sounds that can be sustained. The sustained sounds initially act as a kind of background wash against which the percussion instruments splash their sparkling, exotic sounds (the group includes cimbalom, mandolin and tubular bells) like a calligraphic pictogram. As individual moments occur, different instruments obtrude and new perspectives are revealed in what Paul Griffiths has described as "a free, fluid concatenation of luminescent events."

Éclat was written in 1965 but, as with many Boulez works, it has subsequently been revised and may yet have further modifications. *Multiples* (1970), an extension to *Éclat*, supplements the group of sustaining instruments with ten violas and a basset horn. The sound is much thicker and heavier and the gestural splashes of colour have been replaced by a greater sense of direction, and even a hint of melody. An Oriental dimension is present in both parts of *Éclat / Multiples – Multiples*, in particular, has something of the violent beauty of Japanese Noh theatre.

In 1974 the death of the Italian composer and conductor Bruno Maderna prompted Boulez to write a piece as a memorial to his friend and colleague. *Rituel in memoriam Bruno Maderna* is perhaps Boulez's most direct and approachable work, despite its repetitive nature and its austerity. Boulez has described the work as a "litany for an imaginary ceremonial; a ceremonial of remembrance – whence these recurrent patterns, changing in profile and perspective; a ceremonial of death – ritual of the ephemeral and eternal." In *Rituel* Boulez is clearly interested in a hieratic and formal expression of grief rather than an emotional one. Almost uniquely in his work, *Rituel* has a regular pulse – spread across a battery of unpitched percussion – that signifies not so much a funeral march as a complex and concentrated religious event.

Detractors of Boulez (and of much modern music) are usually those for whom music has to have melody, a regular beat and a clear development. Boulez's work demands a different kind of listening which he has described (apropos *Éclat*) as "a contemplative attitude towards the phenomenon of sonority . . . attentive to what is happening within the resonance itself." This is definitely not easy listening or background music, but demands a committed response for it to make any kind of sense. Boulez's recordings of his own work reinforce the music's underlying poise, balance, clarity and, above all, its dazzlingly vivid sound-world.

Johannes Brahms

Clarinet Quintet; String Quartet, Op. 51 No. 1

Busch Quartet; Reginald Kell (clarinet)

EMI CDH7 64932 2; mid-price

If Brahms had written nothing but chamber music, he would still be ranked as one of the greatest composers of the nineteenth century. No other composer, save Beethoven, wrote so ambitiously or so richly for so wide a range of instrumental groupings. Yet much of Brahms's chamber music has a complexity and textural density that often makes it seem like orchestral music in miniature – a characteristic that led Schoenberg to orchestrate the *Piano Quintet*. On the other hand a profoundly lyrical strand is also evident in a lot of these works, particularly those in which one instrument has a dominant role.

Brahms had not composed anything for about a year when, in 1891, he visited his friend the Duke of Saxe-Meiningen and heard the court orchestra's principal clarinettist Richard Mühlfeld. Brahms was inspired by Mühlfeld's playing, in much the same way that Mozart had been by Anton Stadler's (see p.111), and in the same year he wrote two works for him – the *Clarinet Trio* and the *Clarinet Quintet*, one of his greatest masterpieces, in which Brahms exploits the clarinet's warm velvety tone to create a work with an overriding mood that is autumnal and valedictory.

The *Clarinet Quintet* is not a virtuoso work: clarinet and strings are closely integrated, especially in the first movement, where the improvisatory main theme flows effortlessly between the five voices. The solo instrument comes more to the fore in the central section of the Adagio where, following a hazy, heavy-lidded opening theme, it pours forth a glorious cascade of notes in a rhapsodic style that hints at the Hungarian gypsy music Brahms loved so much. A short movement follows that should be a Scherzo but is more of a wistful folk song with a frisky middle section, and Brahms continues to defy tradition by having a set of variations as his finale, rather than the lively rush that convention demands. Each instrument gets a chance to shine before a sudden stop leads to a subdued version of the quintet's opening theme – an ending that re-establishes the work's elegiac atmosphere.

The *String Quartet No. 1* is an earlier work and is more rugged in character than the *Clarinet Quintet*. The first movement is turbulent, with an undercurrent of disquiet exemplified by the restless rising theme and the rushing quavers which propel the movement forward. The slow movement is equally dark, its strangely suspended atmosphere generated by hesitant, short-breathed phrases. As in the quintet, the next movement is a kind of anti-scherzo – a languid opening section leading to a melodically stronger and more luxuriant one, while the finale – like the first movement – is more concerned with momentum and atmosphere than with melody.

Brahms's chamber works, like much of his music, can sound clogged and heavy-footed in all but the most brilliant of performances. The *Clarinet Quintet* gets such a performance on this disc. There's a fluidity and an ease on display here which is completely captivating. Both Reginald Kell and Adolf Busch, the Busch Quartet's leader, have the ability to make their instruments sing, partly by the discreet use of expressive devices – swooping on the strings, a flexible attitude to the music's pulse – which are now thought of as old-fashioned but which actually give the music a light and shade that brings it alive. The *Quartet* was recorded in 1932, the *Quintet* in 1937 which means that the string sound, especially in the *Quartet*, is a little harsh in the upper register – but it's a small price to pay for music-making of such rare vitality.

Johannes Brahms /
Pyotr Il'yich Tchaikovsky

Violin Concertos

Jascha Heifetz; Chicago Symphony Orchestra; Fritz Reiner (conductor)

RCA 09026 61495 2; mid-price

If the piano was the supreme instrument of Romantic self-expression, then the violin wasn't far behind. In the nineteenth century, every violin virtuoso that emerged was guaranteed music from composers eager to shed glory on themselves and the performer alike. Brahms's *Violin Concerto* was written in 1878 for the outstanding Hungarian violinist Joseph Joachim, who, as one of his closest friends, was on hand to offer technical advice when it was needed.

Joachim's playing was renowned more for its lyricism than for its virtuosity, and Brahms's concerto reflects this. It opens with a long, leisurely orchestral introduction before the violin injects a degree of passion into the proceedings. There's an ongoing sense of orchestral stateliness, but the soloist displays a wide range of feelings from defiance to a brooding melancholy, exemplified by a sombre three-note phrase built up in chords. The slow movement starts with another introduction, this time led by an exquisite oboe solo which is embellished by the violin with increasingly elaborate ornamentation. The finale is a sparkling Rondo, inflected by gypsy music rhythms (a homage to Joachim's Hungarian background), which calls for the bow to be bounced on the strings. Brahms marked it "Allegro giocoso" (fast and cheerful) to which Joachim added "ma non troppo vivace [but not too lively] – otherwise difficult."

Tchaikovsky's *Violin Concerto*, written in the same year as the Brahms, had a more complicated genesis. Recovering from the mental breakdown precipitated by his marriage, the composer was staying near Lake Geneva when a visit by a young violinist called Iosif Kotek – a former pupil of Joachim – inspired him to write his *Violin Concerto* in less than a month. Tchaikovsky then offered it to leading violinist Leopold Auer, who declared it "unviolinistic" and unplayable. When the concerto was finally premiered in 1891 by Adolph Brodsky it was condemned by critic Eduard Hanslick as "barbarously awful! – the violin is no longer played but torn asunder!"

It's true that, when compared to the Brahms, Tchaikovsky's concerto is more of a showpiece. While there's always a certain reserve with Brahms, Tchaikovsky is emotionally unhibited to an extreme degree. The warmly luxuriant opening violin theme soars to an increasingly high level of excitement culminating in its bold statement as a triumphant polonaise for the full orchestra. The kind of mournful folk-style melody that Tchaikovsky could turn out at will dominates the slow movement Canzonetta with some exceptionally delicate exchanges between soloist and woodwind. The explosive finale follows without a break, the orchestra and soloist letting rip in the fieriest of Russian dances with only a brief let-up provided by the second subject – a gypsy-like phrase in the violin over a rustic orchestral drone.

Eventually Leopold Auer relented and became a great champion of Tchaikovsky's concerto. Auer was also a renowned teacher and it's his most famous pupil, Jascha Heifetz, who plays both concertos on this disc. Technically beyond criticism, Heifetz was sometimes berated for a lack of real feeling, but it's hard to understand why when you hear these stupendous performances from the mid-1950s. Both concertos are played with enormous chutzpah: the Brahms, taken considerably faster than most rival versions, has rarely sounded fresher or so alive. Heifetz's phrasing in the slow movement has a spontaneity and a charm that is almost throwaway, and he's supported by some exquisite playing from the Chicago Symphony Orchestra – the woodwind in particular. The Tchaikovsky is no less exciting, full of breathtaking passage work and the most beautiful singing tone, especially in the Canzonetta.

Johannes Brahms

Symphony No. 4

Vienna Philharmonic Orchestra; Carlos Kleiber (conductor)

Deutsche Grammophon 457 706-2; mid-price

Brahms did not get round to completing his first symphony until 1876, when he was 43. His reticence was partly due to the critical drubbing given to his *Piano Concerto No. 1* but also because he was overawed by the example of Beethoven, whose position at the centre of the Austro-German symphonic tradition he wished to emulate. The success of *Symphony No. 1* (dubbed by critics "Beethoven's Tenth") was a great boost to his confidence – a second symphony followed the next year, and a further two in 1883 and 1885.

Brahms's aesthetic position had been established in opposition to the freer, more progressive music of composers like Liszt and Wagner, and his four symphonies reflect this. Each of them conforms to the classic four-movement pattern and themes are developed in a clearly defined way. But, within these restrictions, the music is frequently passionate and deeply lyrical, while avoiding the wilder flights of Romantic excess.

The *Symphony No. 4* is the greatest of Brahms's symphonies, comprising four perfectly proportioned movements, immensely rich in thematic material, which culminate in a brilliant Bach-inspired set of variations – perhaps the most inventive movement in his entire output. The gloriously expansive opening Allegro successfully combines both order and mystery. Its opening theme, based on a sequence of descending thirds, has an other-worldly, elegiac feel. A brief fanfare-like figure introduces the second subject, a upwardly surging tune for horns and cellos that is almost immediately replaced by a sunnier melody for wind. If the Allegro has a sense of nostalgic reminiscence to it, then the Andante is more austere: brass and wind carry a simple melody over pizzicato strings like a march with no real direction. An achingly tender string melody introduces a greater degree of feeling that seems to suggest a mood of pious contemplation.

The next movement, an ebullient Scherzo, shows Brahms at his most carefree and spirited. It's a dance in all but name – albeit a rather heavy-footed one – with a definite sense of bucolic abandon to it. The finale that follows (marked "energico e passionato") reveals Brahms's deep-rooted interest in the music of Bach. It takes the form of a Passacaglia, a Baroque form in which continuous variations are developed around a slow theme, in triple time, played over a repeated bass line. Brahms's theme seems to have been inspired by a section of *Bach's Cantata No. 150* and by his *Chaconne in D minor* for solo violin (Chaconnes and Passacaglias were virtually identical), which Brahms described as "a whole world of the deepest and most powerful expression". In Brahms's thirty variations the constant presence of the ascending theme is distributed throughout the orchestra and embellished in the most original and unexpected ways. The result is a dazzling rollercoaster ride of transformations, in which a delicate flute solo can blend into soaring, effusive string writing in a matter of seconds.

There's no doubt that Brahms suffers more than most at the hands of his interpreters. It's not difficult to make his music sound stodgy, pedantic and even boring. Carlos Kleiber's 1980 recording of *Symphony No. 4* seems dedicated to achieving the opposite effect. It's a thrilling performance that exudes a total sense of belief in the music, from the delicately weighted lilt of its opening bars to its monumental conclusion. The Vienna Philharmonic respond to Kleiber's direction with evident enthusiasm and the final Passacaglia is an electrifying *tour de force*. Kleiber has no qualms about employing extreme dynamic contrasts in this movement and the result has an unstoppable momentum and dramatic thrust.

Max Bruch

Violin Concerto No. 1; Scottish Fantasy

Jascha Heifetz (violin); New Symphony Orchestra of London; Malcolm Sargent (conductor)

RCA 09026 61745 2; with Vieuxtemps, Concerto *No. 5*; mid-price

Max Bruch was a prolific composer, a more than competent conductor and a highly respected teacher, and yet for most of his long professional career he was dogged by the phenomenal success of just one work, his *Violin Concerto No. 1* of 1868. Despite his writing two more violin concertos (not to mention symphonies, operas and oratorios), the first concerto was always the one that the public wanted to hear and violinists wanted to play. Its success assumed nightmarish qualities. Bruch wrote of a trip to Naples in 1903: "On the corner of the Via Toledo they stand there, ready to break out with my first violin concerto as soon as I allow myself to be seen."

Although its success was practically instant, the concerto had taken Bruch four years, and a great deal of effort, to write. Technical advice came from the violinist Joseph Joachim, who was extremely encouraging, and the conductor Hermann Levi, who was not – he disparaged the work for its structural shortcomings. Bruch's most original idea was to write the first movement as a Prelude to the ensuing Adagio rather than as a completely autonomous movement. It begins with a series of quiet exchanges between orchestra and soloist, the violin tentative at first and then more confident in its main theme, which is stated over a tense orchestral backgound of timpani and tremolando strings. It's an exciting opening movement, alternating between the sweeter, more relaxed quality of the violin's second theme and a recurrent tension generated by the interval of a minor third and a restless short-long rhythmic motif. A moment of calm leads into the Adagio, in which the influence of Mendelssohn is clearly apparent in the subdued but powerful emotion of the main theme. Like Brahms ten years later, Bruch closes the concerto with an energetic Hungarian-style Allegro, perhaps a gesture towards the Hungarian-born Joachim, the work's dedicatee and first performer.

Bruch's only other work to approach the first concerto in popularity is the *Scottish Fantasy* of 1880. Inspired (inevitably) by the writings of Sir Walter Scott, the four-movement piece quotes a number of Scottish folk songs and is scored for violin and orchestra, with a prominent harp part to give it a suitably "bardic" feel. Its Scottishness is about as authentic as *Brigadoon*, but it's highly enjoyable if you surrender yourself to its kitsch charms. A gloomy processional opening, from which the wavering violin line emerges, conjures up a kind of misty "days of yore" atmosphere before the soloist lets rip with a heart-tugging version of the song "Auld Robbie Morris". It's followed by a lively dance over a bagpipe-style orchestral drone, a relatively restrained slow movement, and a rousing finale with some spectacularly acrobatic writing for the soloist.

The Scottish Fantasy needs a performer of enormous panache and great skill to prevent it from sounding like cliché-ridden hokum. Jascha Heifetz displays considerably more than that in this scintillating performance from the early '60s. Many great violinists have something of the singing voice about their playing, especially in the Romantic repertoire. With Heifetz almost every aspect of his performance has a "vocal" quality – the way the tone quality can suddenly change to give a new emphasis, the unerring sense of line, and, in particular, the subtle way he will slightly distort the rhythm of a phrase to create a sense of thinking out loud. In the concerto, with its gloriously extended melodies, these qualities are displayed to sensational effect. The disc also includes Vieuxtemps' short *Violin Concerto No. 5*, which not even Heifetz can prevent from sounding like meretricious flim-flam.

Anton Bruckner

Symphony No. 7

Berlin Philharmonic; Herbert von Karajan (conductor)

Deutsche Grammophon 439 037-2; full price

Bruckner began his professional life as an organist and a writer of church music – first at the monastery of St Florian and then at the cathedral of Linz – but the defining moment in his development as a composer occurred in 1863 when he heard a performance of Wagner's *Tannhäuser*. His music was transformed by the experience, from the rule-bound and the conventional to the harmonically daring and the monumental. The sheer vastness of Bruckner's ten symphonies and their pervasive air of religious feeling has often led them to be compared to Gothic cathedrals. It's a fitting analogy, for both combine a monolithic solidity with a soaring, aspirational spirit.

Bruckner was a modest man who was extremely susceptible to criticism. In particular, the destructive reviews of the influential critic Eduard Hanslick were a constant thorn in his side after he moved to Vienna in 1868. He experienced no real success as a composer until his *Symphony No. 7*, written when he was nearly 60. Championed by the conductor Artur Nikisch, the symphony was premiered in Leipzig in 1884 and was soon being performed throughout Germany.

Written in four movements, the *Symphony No. 7* has the most enraptured opening of all Bruckner's works. Over tremolando strings a long radiant phrase, played by the cellos and first horn, begins to unfold itself. A second rising theme emerges from the first, still serene but more purposeful than before. This movement exemplifies the amazing clarity with which Bruckner arranges his raw material. Phrases are built as discrete units, often separated by a pause or by a link passage (like an organ improvisation during a service). Different instrumental sounds are placed against each other but rarely blurred, and repetition is used, as in an argument, to reinforce and emphasize. The result is a cumulative power that is frequently overwhelming.

The Adagio was written in anticipation of Wagner's death and is the most moving of the four movements. Four Wagner tubas, an instrument whose sombre, glowing tone lies between that of the horn and the trombone, are used to state the melancholy opening phrase of the first theme, which continues with three defiant chords played by the strings. A meandering linking passage leads to a lyrical second subject – consolation after the intitial gloom. But with the development of the three-chord motif from the opening theme, a mood of extreme tension is generated by the violins' restless, scurrying accompaniment.

A near-demonic energy dominates the strident Scherzo, a typically lively Austrian *Ländler* (a waltz-like dance), which is in marked contrast to the warmth of the trio that accompanies it. The finale takes up the airy pastoral character of the trio and is essentially jubilant – motifs related to the first movement appear but now with a sunnier disposition. Only a leaping brass phrase hardens the mood, but even this builds to a euphoric climax which culminates in the glorious apotheosis of the work's closing bars.

Karajan recorded the seventh symphony more than once, but this 1989 performance with the Vienna Philharmonic is the most incandescent. It is also the most sculpted, with Karajan shaping Bruckner's arching phrases with extraordinary precision. The exactness of his control and the sumptousness of the orchestral tone tend to reinforce the idea of Bruckner the master builder – the first movement in particular has an almost diagrammatic trajectory, with no detail overlooked. But there is also much tenderness in this account, with Karajan achieving real gravity in the Adagio, and an appropriately lighter energy in the last two movements.

Frédéric Chopin

Sonata No. 3 in B minor (Op. 58); twelve Mazurkas

Evgeny Kissin (piano)

RCA 09026 62542 2; full price

Structure and thematic development have long been held up as
the weak areas of Chopin's work,
particularly in longer pieces such
as the three piano sonatas. But
this is to miss the point: these are
quasi-improvisatory works that
are not to be straitjacketed by the
rigours of classical form. The best
of them, the second in B flat
minor (1839) and the third in B
minor (1844), are tumultuous displays of sustained energy: the
second fast and furious (apart from its famous funeral march), the
third epic in scope and more lyrical, and with a huge sweep of
shifting moods and ideas.

In fact the slow movement of *Sonata No. 3* often sounds close
in spirit to the resigned introspection of late Schubert. Its sombre
main theme is followed by a slow rippling figuration in the right
hand which it is tempting to liken to the movement of water,
although Chopin inveighed against such comparisons, complain-
ing, on his final, purgatorial tour of Britain: "I have never yet
played for an Englishwoman without hearing her say 'like
water'." This movement forms the quiet centre of the sonata.
By contrast, the first movement begins with one of the boldest
and most declamatory of openings before an intensely lyrical figure impinges itself, suggesting – however much Chopin might
have hated the notion – the image of sunlight breaking through
the clouds. The main tension of this movement, as in so much of

Chopin, is created by the disjunction between dramatic, bravura passage work and the simple directness of his emotionally charged melodies. The other two movements are a mesmerising Scherzo, demanding the lightest of touches, and a finale of amazing restlessness and power.

Chopin's Polishness always remained immensely important to him, even though the latter half of his life was spent in Paris. The music of Poland permeates many of his compositions, and he often returned to the form of the mazurka, a Polish dance form in triple time with a strongly accented second beat that makes it resemble a kind of lurching waltz. Chopin often used the mazurka to evoke a more elusive, bitter-sweet image of Poland than was projected by the forthright polonaises. Chopin's lover, the writer George Sand, described one set of mazurkas as "worth more than forty novels", and for such short pieces they manage to convey the most subtle range of feelings. *Mazurka No. 3* of Op. 30, for instance, begins with a bold dance-like attack but its constant shifts between major and minor create an elusive mood of underlying sadness. The most original of all the mazurkas is the quietly concentrated *No. 4*, Op. 17, in which an almost awkward gait and the quirkiest of melodies produce something that is quite unnerving in its fragile beauty.

There are many ways of playing Chopin's music. The composer himself was renowned for his extreme rubato (literally "robbed"), an interpretative device whereby rhythm, instead of being applied in strict time, was expressively distorted by shortening some notes and lengthening others. Evgeny Kissin, one of the most prodigiously talented of modern pianists, employs a rather more circumspect approach which seems almost an antidote to the excesses of many who play this repertoire. Though his playing has a wide range of colours, there's a sinewy energy to it which accentuates the music's dynamism and imagination rather than its emotional vacillations. This performance was recorded live at Carnegie Hall in 1993 but the RCA engineers have managed to keep audience noise to a minimum while maintaining a superbly natural sound.

24

Frédéric Chopin

Piano Concerto No. 1 in E minor (Op. 11); Four Nocturnes; Ballade No. 1; Polonaise No. 6

Maurizio Pollini (piano); Philharmonia Orchestra; Paul Kletzki (conductor)

EMI CDM 5 66221 2; mid-price

When Frédéric Chopin arrived in Paris in 1831, what his contemporaries singled out about his playing was the variety of his touch, and the singing quality (or *cantabile*) of his right hand. As a composer Chopin was primarily a miniaturist, infusing his short pieces with an intimate emotional intensity – what the poet Heine described as the "poetry of feeling". When it came to larger works his method was not that different: these were essentially piano display pieces designed to show off the exquisite tenderness of Chopin's own playing, with none of the dynamic interchange between soloist and orchestra that you find in the concertos of Beethoven.

Of the several works for piano and orchestra that he wrote, the two concertos are the most significant. Both were written just before Chopin left his native Poland in 1830, and both show the influence of two earlier pianist-composers, Johann Hummel and John Field, in their emphasis on long unbroken lines in the right hand. The orchestra's role is always subordinate, either accompanying the piano, or providing long introductions that create a sense of expectation before the piano's entrance. *Piano Concerto No. 1* was actually the second to be written and has a markedly grander first movement that alternates a passionate main theme with a delicately lyrical second one. The central Romance, in effect a piano solo with sporadic accompaniment, is quintessential Chopin – an achingly beautiful melody with an air of tender resignation. The concerto concludes with a typical rondo-finale given a markedly Polish flavour by means of the distinctive 2/4 rhythm of the Krakowiak dance.

Maurizio Pollini's perfectly judged performance dates from 1960, the year he won the prestigious Chopin Competition. His approach is unsentimental and combines a strong touch with quicksilver imagination. Pollini's Chopin is full of drama and the first movement contains the most subtle shifts of mood and emphasis. But he never loses sight of the essentially vocal conception of many of the melodic lines, and the main tune of the Romanze is wonderfully phrased. The Romanze is very similar in style to the solo nocturnes, a form that John Field had invented as a lyrical and dreamy short piece with a highly expressive melody in the right hand. Chopin transformed what had been rather languorous and superficial music into something more profound. Pollini plays four of them and once again it's the glassy delicacy of his playing that is so impressive, the way he combines firmness with a sense of the music's fragility.

The disc concludes with two of Chopin's most famous pieces, the *Ballade No. 1* (Op. 23) and the *Polonaise No. 6* (Op. 53). The four *Ballades* are among Chopin's most powerful works, abounding in quite startlingly dramatic contrasts, with moments of lyric tenderness pushed up against passages of tumultuous energy. The narrative implication of the name "ballade" (applied to non-vocal music for the first time) has led some people to link these pieces to the longer poems of Chopin's fellow-Pole Adam Mickiewicz, and, indeed, both share a certain volatile and episodic quality. For Chopin the polonaise – a rather stately national dance – was a vehicle for expressing his impassioned feelings about the plight of his native land. *No. 6* is the most exuberant of all and its dominant mood of bold defiance has earned it the nickname "Heroic". Pollini plays the *Ballade No. 1* with magisterial control building its discreet elements towards a shattering climax; his account of the *Polonaise No. 6* is no less commanding, and reveals the most incisive articulation in the difficult left-hand ostinatos at the centre of the piece.

25

Aaron Copland

Piano Concerto; Symphonic Ode; Appalachian Spring

Lorin Hollander (piano); Seattle Symphony Orchestra; Gerard Schwarz (conductor)

Delos DE 3154; full price

Aaron Copland began his career as a composer with impeccable Modernist credentials. Studying in Paris with Nadia Boulanger – the most advanced music teacher of the day – he was introduced to the work of the Parisian avant-garde and was particularly struck by the clean textures and incisive lines of Stravinsky's neo-classical works. Copland also loved jazz, and the first works of his maturity, written on his return to New York, succeed in marrying the lean textures of neo-classicism with the ebullient syncopation of jazz.

The last of these jazz-influenced works was the *Piano Concerto* of 1926, written one year after Gershwin's *Piano Concerto in F* (see p.72) but without that work's button-holing charm. Copland's two-movement concerto is more angular and abrasive, concerned with rhythm rather than melody. A restrained, almost alienated, mood prevails throughout the first movement, beginning with the opening bluesy fanfare and continuing with the introspective piano writing. In contrast, the second movement is all dash, the piano's syncopations lurching unsteadily before getting into their stride. Copland conceived of his concerto as a dramatic work, and the piano does indeed seem like a character moving through a modern city, negotiating the brash sounds, the bright lights and the jostling crowds.

The *Symphonic Ode*, written a year later for the fiftieth anniversary of the Boston Symphony Orchestra, marks the beginning of a new austerity in Copland's music. An even greater transparency of texture is evident and rhythm is extremely complex. Copland rated the *Ode* among his finest works but he was aware of what he called its "bony" outline, and "softened" it up in a later revision. By the mid-1930s he had changed direction once again. Politicized by the Depression, he had become aware that a "new public for music had grown up around radio and the phonograph. It made no sense to ignore them . . . I felt it was worth the effort to . . . say what I had to say in the simplest possible terms."

Among the numerous creations of this new listener-friendly Copland is his much-loved dance score *Appalachian Spring*. Written for the dancer Martha Graham and completed in 1944, *Appalachian Spring* tells of a newly wedded couple setting up home in Pennsylvania in the early nineteenth century. It's a work that deals, in quasi-mythic terms, with hope and aspiration – both personal and communal – and it struck an immediate chord with American audiences. A true collaboration, Graham's spare but emotional choreography and Isamu Noguchi's minimal setting were perfectly complemented by Copland's understated eloquence. His skill in creating lucid, open textures is combined with strong affirmative melodies, culminating in his extended treatment of the Shaker hymn "Simple Gifts" at the end of the work. A strong sense of wide, open spaces is evoked in Copland's scoring, beginning with a magical depiction of dawn on a spring morning, and a mood of religious fervour and joyous celebration is sustained through energetic dance music that draws on traditional forms like square dancing.

Gerard Schwarz and the Seattle Symphony Orchestra are exemplary interpreters of Copland's music, giving performances that are clean and precise without being ungiving. In the wrong hands *Appalachian Spring* can slide into cuteness, but there's no hint of that here – instead the music comes over as light-filled and visionary. The *Piano Concerto* is equally impressive: Hollander makes the ideal Copland pianist, being discreet and sympathetic in the first movement, and witty rather than aggressive in the lively finale.

26

Arcangelo Corelli

"La Folia" and other sonatas

Purcell Quartet

Hyperion CDA 66266; full price

Though instrumental music was becoming increasingly important by the middle of the seventeenth century, Arcangelo Corelli is nonetheless unusual in that he wrote absolutely no music for the voice. Instead he worked exclusively in the three genres which he helped to establish: the trio sonata, the solo sonata and the concerto grosso. Corelli published little but his influence was enormous: all subsequent composers who worked in these genres used his work as a model.

Corelli was born in Fusignano but he gained his musical education mostly at Bologna, which, alongside Venice, was Italy's most important centre for instrumental music. From 1675 he was based in Rome, where he established himself as one of the city's leading violinists, playing in theatres and in church ensembles. As a performer Corelli was renowned for the elegance and pathos of his playing: "I never met with any man", wrote a contemporary, "that suffered his passions to hurry him away so much whilst he was playing on the violin." His patrons in Rome included Queen Christina of Sweden, Cardinal Pamphili, whose music master he became in 1687, and Cardinal Ottoboni, in whose palace he lived from 1689 almost until his death.

By Corelli's time the term "sonata" – which originally meant music that was played rather than sung – referred to a piece for a small ensemble, in four alternately slow and fast movements. A trio sonata, the principal chamber music genre of the Baroque period, consisted of three parts played by four instruments: two upper parts – usually violins – plus a supporting part (called a continuo) played by a keyboard and a low stringed instrument. A distinction was made between the *sonata da camera* (chamber sonata), which employed dance forms, and the more serious *sonata da chiesa* (church sonata), which usually did not (and wasn't necessarily performed exclusively in a church setting). With Corelli's four published sets of trio sonatas this already vague distinction became even more blurred. All of them are refined and elegant works and what especially impressed his contemporaries was the way the violin parts seemed to mimic the human voice, above all in the slower movements.

The twelve sonatas of Corelli's Opus 5 for solo violin and continuo, which formally resemble the trio sonatas but include an additional fast movement, made an even greater impact on their publication in 1700. Corelli was as influential a performer and teacher of the violin as he was a composer, and these works can be seen as summarizing his understanding of the best qualities of the instrument. Though considerably more virtuosic in the violin part than the trio sonatas, they possess the same classic qualities of tastefulness and easy lyricism. Even in the most technically difficult moments the brilliance of the passage work serves the music rather than the performer.

Corelli is not a composer of passionate extremes like Vivaldi, and to listen to an entire set of his sonatas is to risk being underwhelmed by the sheer good taste of it all. The advantage of this excellent disc is that the Purcell Quartet have picked and chosen some of the highpoints of the different sets, mixing solo sonatas and trio sonatas. Their generally light but lively approach to the music provides the most persuasive account of Corelli on disc. The most famous work – and the most energetic – is the violin sonata that takes the form of a set of sparkling variations on the famous popular dance tune "La Folia". This gets a highly spirited rendition from violinist Elizabeth Wallfisch, who combines a delicate touch with a gutsy attack and enormous flair.

27

Claude Debussy

Images 1 & 2; Children's Corner

Arturo Benedetti Michelangeli (piano)

Deutsche Grammophon 415 372-2; full price

Debussy's piano music reveals the composer's overriding concern with quality of sound rather than with formal argument. There's a sensuous glow and a harmonic originality to the writing which points to sources of inspiration far removed from traditional piano writing. His attraction to old church modes (or scales) gives the harmony its distinctive edge, while his hypnotic repetitions and bell-like sonorities were in part influenced by the Javanese gamelan orchestra that he saw at the Paris World Fair of 1889.

Among the most beguiling of all Debussy's piano works are the two sets of *Images*, each of which consists of three short pieces. *Images I*, written at the same time as *La Mer* (see p.58) begins with a rather less turbulent evocation of water. *Reflets dans l'Eau* (Reflections in the Water) uses a sequence of rich and weighty chords to create a powerful sense of depth and stillness. The *Hommage à Rameau* is a sombre tribute to the eighteenth-century French composer that is decidedly modern in its unpredictable harmonies. The final punningly titled *Mouvement* is Debussy at his most spirited with a moto perpetuo central motif that has all the mesmerizing, centrifugal energy of a spinning top.

Images II is more abstract – despite specific titles – and even more daring in its harmonies. In *Cloches à travers les Feuilles* (Bells through the Leaves) he builds up separate layers of sound – based on simple scale patterns – that emerge and recede as if from different distances. There's a distinctly Eastern feel to the harmonies and slowly shifting chords of the next piece, *Et la Lune Descend sur le Temple qui fut* (And the Moon goes down over the Ruined Temple), which suggests an atmosphere of subdued light and gently chiming bells, though the suggestive title was actually added after the piece was written. The last piece, *Poissons d'Or* (Goldfish), was inspired by a Japanese panel that Debussy kept on his desk. There's a darting, quicksilver energy in evidence here that is briefly undermined by menacing octaves in the bass.

Children's Corner, written for Debussy's daughter Chouchou, is a set of miniatures that brilliantly conjures up the world of the nursery and children's picture books. Debussy peppers the collection with a sophisticated wit – the first piece, *Doctor Gradus ad Parnassum*, parodies the kind of mechanical finger exercises found in piano primers of the early nineteenth century. *Jimbo's Lullaby* and *Serenade for the Doll* are musical tributes to two toys, elephantinely heavy-footed in the first, poetic in the second. Most beautiful of all is the exquisite *The Snow is Dancing* in which a four-note phrase in the right hand is repeated an octave lower and half a beat later in the left hand to create a magical illusion of delicately falling snowflakes. The *Little Shepherd* is a miniaturized *L'après-midi d'un faune* (see p.57) while the final piece, *Golliwog's Cakewalk*, is a lively pastiche of ragtime music which includes a passing dig at Wagner.

Debussy, himself a gifted pianist, worked closely with several younger players to establish something of a tradition of playing his music that emphasized atmosphere, often through much use of the sustaining pedal. Benedetti Michelangeli's scintillating 1971 recording breaks through this tradition through playing that focuses on translucency and has a sharpness of attack in the more dynamic passages. Every strand of the musical argument is laid bare and presented with the most crystalline brilliance. Far from being cold, as some critics have suggested, Benedetti Michelangeli's readings bring out every subtlety and nuance of the music through a combination of astonishing technique and deep sensitivity.

28

Claude Debussy / Maurice Ravel

String Quartets

Cleveland Quartet

Telarc CD-80111; full price

The names of Ravel and Debussy are often linked under the rather generalized heading of Impressionism. It is true that, as students, both reacted against the academicism of the Paris Conservatoire by developing vividly coloured music of great harmonic freedom that was often highly atmospheric and imagistic. But in fact the differences between them are as marked as the similarities: Ravel's music, on the whole, has a harder and more jewel-like surface, Debussy's is more blurred and evanescent. Both men wrote just one string quartet each, and it is in these works that their styles are most congruent — not surprisingly, since Ravel's quartet was consciously modelled on that of his older contemporary.

Debussy wrote his *String Quartet in G minor* in 1893 when he was 31, and it was clearly a significant work for him, since it's the only one to which he assigned an opus number. It is in four movements: two fast ones at either end, an elusive Scherzo for a second movement followed by a slow third movement. Following the example of César Franck (see p.69), Debussy employs cyclical form, which means that the heavy, declamatory opening theme recurs in different manifestations throughout the entire work. But there are also many other themes which come and go with a profligate generosity, including two wistfully lyrical melodies in the first and third movements. The Scherzo is the most dramatic movement, dominated as it is by a strumming accompaniment over which a light but restless melody glides. The slow movement is the most profound: mellow and subdued, with at its heart a folk-like melody of great tenderness.

Debussy was a great inspiration to Ravel and the younger composer's *String Quartet in F major* was, perhaps, intended as a homage to him. It follows the same cyclical pattern, and even has a second movement Scherzo that is propelled along by plucked strings. But Ravel's quartet is longer and seems more concentrated as well as more expansive. It was begun in 1902, the first movement being originally intended as part of a composite work written by four of Fauré's students as a tribute to him. There's a lyricism to the main theme of the first movement that is reminiscent of Fauré in its outgoing and sunny disposition, while the Scherzo has a greater sense of momentum than Debussy's with a second theme that conveys an autumnal mood of quiet regret. It's a mood that spills over into the slow movement, whose prevailing stillness makes the occasionally more animated passages seem all the more dramatic. The finale is fast and furious with a restless energy that borders on the demented. Ironically Fauré, to whom the quartet was dedicated, thought this movement a failure. Debussy was rather more generous: "In the name of the gods of music", he told Ravel, "do not touch a single note of what you have written."

Intriguingly, this recording by the Cleveland Quartet uses four exceptional Stradivarius instruments that once belonged to the great violinist Paganini. What difference this makes to the performance is difficult to quantify, but unquestionably there is an outstanding tonal warmth and a fullness to the sound. The players display a level of interpretative like-mindedness that you only find in the greatest of quartets, and there's a vitality and a freshness to the playing that is entirely appropriate to such formally adventurous music. In the Debussy the plethora of thematic ideas seem to grow out of each other in a completely natural manner while in the Ravel they achieve the perfect balance between poise and passion.

29

Claude Debussy

Prélude à l'après-midi d'un faune; La Mer; Trois Nocturnes

Philharmonia Orchestra; Guido Cantelli (conductor)

Testament SBT 1011; full price

It's become a cliché to date the beginning of modern music to 1894 and the first performance of Debussy's short orchestral work *Prélude à l'après-midi d'un faune* (Prelude to the Afternoon of a Faun), but the originality of this gentle, hypnotic music might not strike you immediately. What's radical about the piece is the way Debussy creates the prevailing mood of dreamy sensuousness through a combination of tonal imprecision (the key signature is never clear) and an extremely vivid use of instrumental colour to provide the most transparent of textures. Inspired by a Mallarmé poem (describing the erotic reveries of a faun) which is itself allusive and imprecise, the music begins with a languorous phrase for flute and horn that snakes its way over a richly varied background – harps and horn initially, then tremolo strings – building gradually in intensity, but pointedly avoiding any conventional thematic development.

Debussy's music is often compared with Impressionism because of its similar concern with atmosphere, but Debussy preferred to identify his work with that of Symbolist poets like Mallarmé and Verlaine. *Nuages* (Clouds), from the *Trois Nocturnes* of 1899, encapsulates his ability to conjure both the physical sensation of natural phenomena and the poeticization of that sensation, as if the experience were filtered through memory or a dream. Debussy described the piece as a rendering of "the unchanging aspect of the sky and the slow, solemn motion of the white clouds" and it's this quality of time suspended that is brilliantly communicated through the most subtle shifts of movement and colour. In contrast, *Fêtes* is an ebullient and celebratory affair that conveys all the energy and joy of a festive crowd. The third piece, *Sirènes*, is disappointing; the idea was to suggest the rhythms of the sea and the mysterious song of the sirens, but the result is strangely mechanical, and even a little kitsch.

A more convincing depiction of the sea can be found in Debussy's greatest orchestral work, *La Mer* (The Sea), composed at Eastbourne in the summer of 1904. It's a tightly constructed work with thematic connections between its three movements, but the main impact comes from the way it communicates a feeling of elemental force – even at its most restful moments a sense of power is never far away. It is the mutability of the natural world that Debussy found so attractive, and in each movement he homes in on different and specific qualities. The first movement, *De l'aube à midi sur la mer* (From Dawn till Noon on the Sea), seems concerned with the myriad transformations of light on water; the second, *Jeux de vagues* (Play of the Waves), is lighter and more restless in character; while the third, *Dialogue du vent et de la mer* (Dialogue of the Wind and the Sea) unleashes the full fury of a storm at sea.

Guido Cantelli was established as one of the finest conductors of his generation when he was killed in a plane crash at the early age of 38. Fortunately he had already made several recordings, of which his Debussy sessions with the Philharmonia Orchestra are outstanding. Recorded in mono in the mid-1950s they still sound absolutely fresh, owing in no small part to Cantelli's obsessive attention to detail. In every piece on this disc, questions of instrumental balance – so vital in Debussy's orchestral music – have been perfectly judged to maximize the subtlety of the colouration and the internal drama of the music. So sure is Cantelli's touch, that he even manages to make the second-rate *Le Martyre de Saint-Sébastien* sound exciting.

30

Josquin Desprez

Missa Pange Lingua

Ensemble Clément Janequin; Ensemble Organum; Marcel Pérès (director)

Harmonia Mundi HMC 901239; full price

Although Josquin Desprez (c.1440–1521) dominated the musical landscape of Western Europe during his lifetime, very little is known about him. He was almost certainly a native of the Picardy region of France but spent most of his career in Italy (in Milan, Rome and Ferrara), where his fame was unrivalled, despite a reputation for irascibility. Contemporaries compared him to Michelangelo, and Martin Luther memorably said of him: "Josquin is master of the notes, which do what he wants, while other composers must do what the notes want."

Polyphony – the art of creating a complex web of sound through the combination of separate lines of music – came of age with Josquin: he consolidated the achievements of his predecessors, turning their essentially linear style into something more harmonically complex and expressive. To an unprecedented degree attention was paid to conveying the meaning of words through the music, but it is the sheer beauty of the sound which is the most striking feature of Josquin's music. It was Josquin who established the pattern for Renaissance sacred music, with rich vocal textures made up of long arching phrases, in which consistent imitation between the voices creates a sense both of unity and of progression. It was a style of sacred music that was to reach the height of its achievement in the gloriously fervent Masses of Victoria (see p.195).

Though Josquin wrote a substantial amount of courtly songs, it is as a composer of motets and of around eighteen masses that he exerted the widest influence. The four-part *Missa Pange Lingua*, one of his last and best-known masses, was written around 1515 for the feast of Corpus Christi. It's a work of pared-down but highly expressive intensity, in which he employs the well-established technique of creating the music around an already existing tune (the *cantus firmus*) – in this case the plainsong Corpus Christi hymn, "Pange Lingua". However, rather than emphasize the borrowed material (which is what his contemporaries tended to do), Josquin treats the plainsong melody very freely and largely disguises it within the overall musical fabric by distributing it between the different voices, which he combines with great variety and with an acute sensitivity to the text. The most striking instance of this occurs in the Credo where the lively interplay of lines suddenly ceases at the section beginning "et incarnatus est" (and was incarnate) which are sung homophonically, that is with all the voices moving together as one. This creates a sudden change of mood from the celebratory to the solemn and was to become a commonplace device in future settings of the Credo.

Variety is very much the key to this 1986 recording, with the two combined all-male choirs giving a splendidly dynamic performance. As well as the fixed parts of the mass composed by Josquin (the Kyrie, Gloria, Credo, Sanctus and Agnus) you also hear plainsong settings of the parts specific to the feast of Corpus Christi, including the hymn on which the mass is based. This has the effect both of placing Josquin's music within a larger liturgical context and of highlighting the rich splendour of the polyphony. Matters of speed, volume and, above all, attack are very much attuned to the meaning of the words, so that instead of the usual pious serenity that you so often find in performances of Renaissance polyphony, you get something much more expressive and passionate, with the ritual of the mass being consciously connected to the human aspect of the Christian story.

31

Antonín Dvořák

Cello Concerto in E minor

Mstislav Rostropovich (cello); Berlin Philharmonic; Herbert von Karajan (conductor)

Deutsche Grammophon 447 413-2; mid-price

Given the cello's suitability to passionate utterance, it's odd that the nineteenth century – the century of Romanticism – produced only three cello concertos of any distinction: the *Concerto No. 1* of Saint-Saëns and those by Schumann and Dvořák. Of these three, the Dvořák concerto, written in America in 1894, is certainly the most popular and arguably the finest. Like Elgar in his cello concerto, Dvořák homes in on the instrument's mellow-toned eloquence, producing a work that is tender and filled with nostalgic reminiscences of his native Bohemia. "Why on earth didn't I know one could write a cello concerto like this?" was Brahms's response. "If I had only known I would have written one years ago."

Perhaps even more oddly, Dvořák had begun and abandoned a cello concerto thirty years earlier, and only re-awoke to the lyric potential of such a work after hearing a performance of the *Cello Concerto No. 2* by Victor Herbert, best known as a composer of Broadway operettas. The profoundly personal tone of Dvořák's concerto is explained by the fact that during its early stages he received news that his sister-in-law and early love, Josefina Kaunitzová, was dying. His response was to take the melody of her favourite of his songs, "Leave Me Alone", and introduce it into the middle section of the slow movement. He subsequently re-wrote the finale to incorporate more of the song when he heard of Josefina's death.

The concerto's tendency to fluctuate between a passive mood of sombre regret and a passionate yearning is evident in the long orchestral introduction with which it begins. Hushed woodwind state the initial motif, the strings develop a degree of tension and excitement, a French horn asserts the tender second subject and, shortly after, the soloist enters with all the intensity of an animal straining at a leash. With the soloist's reprise of the horn tune the cello's vocalizing quality comes into its own, and it does so even more thrillingly when the initial theme is developed, very softly, in the minor key.

Calm tranquillity marks the start of the Adagio, the concerto's most poignant movement. Again the woodwind introduce the first theme, which has something of a church procession about it. The cello increases a mood of restrained grief which is suddenly broken into by loud and portentous trombones – the cue for the cello to begin the ardent "Josefina" theme. Throughout this movement the cello is like a mourner at a funeral, initially all quiet dignity but gradually unable to control its grief. Even in the fast Rondo-finale the sense of loss is maintained with a rest-less, questing solo part that ranges from febrile intensity to quiet acceptance. In a brilliant touch, the "song" theme re-appears just before the end to establish a brief moment of transcendence. The concerto's dedicatee, cellist Hanus Wihan, added a cadenza to the last movement but Dvořák removed it, explaining that he wanted the work to close "gradually, like a sigh".

One of the concerto's greatest modern exponents is the Russian cellist Mstislav Rostropovich who has played it on a number of highly charged occasions, including a performance, in London, on the day after Russian tanks rolled into Prague. This recording dates from the same period and matches the unbridled power and passion of Rostropovich with the opulence of the Berlin Philharmonic under Karajan. The result is one of the most lushly romantic performances on disc, but with the muscular tone of Rostropovich preventing a slide into indulgence. The *Rococo Variations* for cello and orchestra, Tchaikovsky's elegant homage to the eighteenth century, gets an equally full-blooded treatment.

32

Antonín Dvořák

Symphonies Nos. 8 & 9

Berlin Philharmonic; Rafael Kubelík (conductor)

Deutsche Grammophon 447 412-2; mid-price

Bohemia, where Dvořák was born in 1841, is today the westernmost region of the Czech Republic, but in the nineteenth century it was still part of the Austrian Empire. For Czechs, their indigenous music became an important vehicle of national consciousness, and Dvořák (like Smetana before him) strove to give a Czech colouring to his work by incorporating folk material and employing specifically Czech subject matter. At the same time, he assimilated the ethnic character of his music into an Austro-German musical style, and there is a strong kinship between his music and that of his contemporary (and admirer) Brahms.

Dvořák's early symphonies are engaging but derivative, and it was not until the fifth symphony that his own voice emerged. By 1889, the year of *Symphony No. 8*, he was not only in complete command of his material but wishing "to write a work which is different from my other symphonies, with individual ideas worked out in a new way". This "new way" can be heard in the symphony's first two movements, where themes are developed in a more episodic fashion, with the orchestration often divided into smaller chamber-like groups. It was a method that was to influence Mahler, though in Dvořák's hands it has none of Mahler's volatility and anxiety. Indeed the eighth symphony is one of Dvořák's most exuberant and sunny works, with a long slow movement like a genial, pastoral narrative, and a Scherzo in which a wistful waltz is given a decidedly folkish twist. The finale is more straightforward, with a set of variations on a "big tune" that is reminiscent of Brahms but with more bounce and a clearer texture.

In 1892 Dvořák left his native land for America, where he was to head the newly founded New York National Conservatory for three years. While there he developed a passion for American music, particularly the songs of Stephen Foster and Negro spirituals. He also showed an interest in Native American music, although his comments suggest that what he heard bore little or no resemblance to the real thing. One result of all this was his *Symphony No. 9* (*"From the New World"*), which abounds in melodies showing a strong American influence, most famously the haunting cor anglais theme of the slow movement, which sounds like a spiritual and was scored for cor anglais in order to imitate the voice of the black student who sang for Dvořák at the conservatory. The symphony was an immediate success and has proved to be Dvořák's most popular work. Although scholars point to its structural weaknesses and the slightly mechanical way themes are developed, this rather misses the point – the "New World" is a symphony of the most astonishing melodic fecundity which succeeds in conjuring up a vividly expansive impression of the composer's New World.

Rafael Kubelík, one of the greatest of Czech conductors, spent half his life in exile, only returning to his homeland in 1990 after the collapse of Communism. His performances were famed for their combination of high energy and emotional intensity, never more so when he was conducting Dvořák. In conjunction with the Berlin Philharmonic he produced the most electrifying versions of these symphonies on disc. The eighth boasts some exceptionally fine sectional playing from the orchestra but is most notable for its tremendous warmth and engaging *joie de vivre*. In the "*New World*" Kubelík seems to relish the directness of Dvořák's feelings but his vitality means that sentimentality is avoided. This is a pulsating, thrilling account with even the more meandering parts of the finale injected with a sense of purpose and direction.

33

Edward Elgar

Cello Concerto; Sea Pictures

Jacqueline du Pré (cello); Janet Baker (mezzo-soprano); London
Symphony Orchestra; John Barbirolli (conductor)

EMI CDC5 56806 2; full price

In some circles the music of Sir
Edward Elgar is still equated with
the pomp and swagger of
Edwardian England. Even when
the music is sombre in tone, this is
put down to the composer's sadness at the passing of an Imperial
golden age. Such a picture has
some truth but creates too limited
an impression of his achievement,
for Elgar was no little-Englander.
He identified with the musical tradition of Schumann and
Brahms, and forced English music out of the inertia and
parochialism in which it had been stuck for most of the nineteenth century.

The *Cello Concerto,* written in 1919, is Elgar's last masterpiece, though he lived for a further fifteen years. Along with
the other music he wrote in the aftermath of World War I, it
has a profoundly introspective and melancholy strain. Its success
was not immediate (the first performance was disastrously
under-rehearsed) but it's now the most popular of all his works.
Its opening is dramatic: thick, bold chords from the soloist,
with the lightest of accompaniments, leads to a tentative
ascending phrase from the cello before the simple, lilting main
theme is introduced by the violas. The overall mood is wistful
and subdued even after the appearance of a more sprightly second theme. The reappearance of the cello's opening flourish –
this time played pizzicato – paves the way for a short but

skittishly energetic Scherzo, though even here there are undertones of agitation.

Throughout the concerto Elgar's scoring is deft and economic, nowhere more so than in the Adagio, where the soloist is the dominant voice in a great outpouring of grief and yearning that gradually intensifies. It is followed by an Allegro, the longest and liveliest movement of the four, with a vigorous main theme that seems to contain elements both of joy and of anger. A more agonized tone is established in the second half with a slower theme like a cry from the heart. The cello's opening chords reappear defiantly towards the end before the work rushes to its conclusion.

Elgar was not a particularly distinguished songwriter, but he excelled himself in *Sea Pictures*, the cycle of five songs that he wrote for contralto and orchestra (premiered in 1899, and later championed by Mahler). Here his orchestral writing effectively represents the ocean's powerful presence through several highly imaginative touches – from the heavy chords conveying the swell of the sea in the first song, to the storm-tossed fervour of the last. The choice of verses is typically Edwardian: a mixture of over-wrought religiosity (*Sabbath Morning at Sea*), bombast (*The Swimmer*), a touch of fairy-land (*Sea Slumber Song*), and sentimental whimsy (*Where Corals Lie*). But Elgar manages to raise his material into something genuinely moving, nowhere more so than in the simple directness with which he sets his wife Alice's poem *In Haven*.

The huge popularity of the *Cello Concerto* (especially in England) is largely due to Jacqueline du Pré who, in her short career, virtually made it her own. Du Pré played the work with such passion and febrile intensity that it seemed to open up new vistas of feeling. In Sir John Barbirolli (a fellow cellist), she had a conductor completely in accord with her vision of the piece and the result has become a benchmark for all subsequent interpreters. To a slightly lesser extent Janet Baker's account of *Sea Pictures* has achieved a similar status. There is something of the cello in the velvety warmth of Baker's voice and every word is expressed with palpable sincerity.

34

Gabriel Fauré

Requiem

Agnès Mellon (soprano), Peter Kooy (baritone); La Chapelle Royale; Les Petits Chanteurs de Saint-Louis; Ensemble Musique Oblique; Philippe Herreweghe (conductor)

Harmonia Mundi HMC 901292; full price

Of the two outstanding Requiem masses written in the nineteenth century, Verdi's is big, noisy and apocalyptic, while Fauré's – most of which was composed in early 1888, shortly after the death of his mother – is low-key, reassuring and consolatory. Significantly, Fauré dispensed altogether with the Dies Irae, the long sequence (or hymn) about the Day of Judgement which Verdi made the centre-piece of his work. The differences between the two works are differences of temperament and of intent: Verdi clearly conceived his *Requiem* for the concert hall whereas Fauré's is for church use (it was first performed at the Paris church of La Madeleine, where he was organist) and has an unmistakable aura of candles and incense to it.

Fauré's early training was at the École Niedermeyer, a Paris music school with a bias towards ecclesiastical music, and in much of his music, including the *Requiem*, there are hints of the church modes that he would have learned there. Both the Introit ("Requiem aeternam") and the opening of the Offertory possess a chant-like quality and throughout the work the harmonies often take on an archaic simplicity. There's a similarly direct and unfussy quality to the solos that intersperse the choruses, most notably the pure and ethereal Pie Jesu, which was originally sung by a boy soprano from the Madeleine choir. In the Sanctus a solo violin weaves an ornate pattern over gently rippling strings as sopranos and tenors pass a simple phrase back and forth between them. The overwhelming impression of comforting serenity is most marked in the Agnus Dei, whose expansive opening string phrase is reminiscent of the well-known lullaby in Fauré's children's piece *The Dolly Suite*. A darker note occurs towards the end of the Agnus setting with the repetition of the words "Requiem aeternam" and the introduction of trombones.

The two-note motif on alternate beats that accompanies the baritone solo in the Libera Me suggests the beating of a heart, and there's an element of anxiety to this section that reaches a climax with a subdued kettledrum roll – like a distant and ominous clap of thunder – on the words "Dies irae" (day of wrath). Calm is restored in the delightful In Paradisum, whose bubbling organ ostinato conjures up an underwater realm of disembodied spirits and seems to conform to Fauré's vision of death as "a happy deliverance, an aspiration towards the happiness of the hereafter, rather than a painful passing away."

One of the most innovative features of Fauré's *Requiem* is its orchestration, in which there are no violins and woodwind – instead the warmly mellow sound is achieved through divided violas and cellos, harp and organ, with trumpets, horns, trombones and kettledrums added to give a darker and occasionally more assertive tone. At the request of Fauré's publisher, the *Requiem* was later re-scored for full orchestra, and that is the version most commonly used today. On this exquisite recording, however, Philippe Herreweghe uses an edition of the work which goes back to Fauré's original scoring, and the advantages in terms of clarity and the rich velvety sound produced, makes the later symphonic scoring seem redundant. Herreweghe has paid a lot of attention to getting the balance between his forces absolutely right. The soloists are not big-voiced "stars", but Agnès Mellon's fervent and restrained delivery of the Pie Jesu blends just perfectly with the autumnal sound of the strings. The *Requiem* is paired with the charming but conventional *Messe des Pêcheurs de Villerville*, an early work (written in collaboration with Messager) for female choir and chamber orchestra.

35

César Franck

Sonata for Violin and Piano

Itzhak Perlman (violin), Vladimir Ashkenazy (piano)

Decca 452 887-2; mid-price

In his novel *Swann's Way* Marcel Proust describes the sensations awoken in the mind of his protagonist Swann on hearing a violin sonata by the composer Vinteuil. In a long and brilliantly sustained passage, Proust maps the correlation between the sound that music makes and the thoughts and associations that are triggered by it. In Swann's case, the reminder of a failing love affair leads to a meditation on the nature of music itself. Vinteuil was an invented character, but it is generally thought that the inspiration for the music came from the *Violin Sonata* of César Franck, one of the most voluptuous and beguiling of all nineteenth-century chamber works.

The *Sonata* was written in 1886, just four years before Franck's death. It is part of a late flowering in his music that seems to have been prompted by his unrequited infatuation with fellow composer, and legendary beauty, Augusta Holmès. Before his friendship with Holmès, Franck specialized in rather earnest religious music, but in the last decade of his life his music took on a more sensuous quality and a greater adventurousness.

In much of his music Franck favoured a method of ordering his material called cyclical form, whereby a musical motif, or cell, undergoes various subtle transformations throughout a work's successive movements, reaching its most complete development in the finale. At the start of the *Sonata*, after a soothing four-bar phrase from the piano, the violin's first theme grows from a small lilting motif into a luxuriant melody that extends itself, like an endless song, over 27 bars. The movement's more plaintive second subject is reserved exclusively for the piano. Originally Franck wanted this movement played slowly, but the work's dedicatee, the violinist Eugène Ysaÿe, persuaded him that it worked better at a brisker tempo, while still retaining the same mood of serenity. In contrast, the Allegro starts off with a storm of turbulent semiquavers from the piano before being joined by the violin. Despite moments of introspective repose, this is the sonata's most agitated movement – passionate and wildly rhapsodic.

The Recitativo-fantasia that follows has a markedly improvisatory feel to it, the violin revisiting old ground in a mood of dreamy speculation. A sense of order is restored by the finale in which the calmest, most dignified of themes is played in canon, that is both instruments playing the same melody but with the violin starting a few beats after the piano. It's the kind of tricky formal exercise that one associates with Bach, but Franck carries it off brilliantly, repeating the theme four times with material from the previous movements interspersed between the repeats.

This is a work that calls for two evenly balanced and completely sympathetic performers. Itzhak Perlman and Vladimir Ashkenazy fit the bill perfectly. Perlman is incapable of producing anything but a beautiful sound – indeed his sweet and centred tone can sometimes sound cloying, but it never does so in this performance. More than most, he treats Franck's gloriously long-breathed phrases like song. His sense of line, subtle shifts in pace and dynamics have all the naturalness and control of a great opera singer. The piano sound is not as well captured as the violin but Ashkenazy is the most sensitive of partners, bold and eloquent but never overwhelming the violin sound. On this disc both artists combine with horn player Barry Tuckwell in the Brahms *Horn Trio*, an unusual mixture of instruments which works suprisingly well, especially in the elegiac slow movement.

36

George Gershwin

Rhapsody in Blue; Piano Concerto in F; An American in Paris

London Symphony Orchestra; André Previn (pianist/conductor)

EMI CDM 5 66891 2; mid-price

By the early 1920s, jazz – hitherto a music of black Americans – was being re-fashioned (some would say diluted) in order to make it more acceptable to a larger, mainly white, audience. The leading figure in this "popularization" of jazz was the classically trained band leader Paul Whiteman. In 1924, in a bid for even greater respectability, Whiteman organized a "jazz" concert at a classical venue, and asked George Gershwin – a successful composer of Broadway musicals – to write a concerto for piano and jazz orchestra. The result, *Rhapsody in Blue*, was the undoubted highpoint in a very bizarre programme that included popular hits like "Yes, We Have No Bananas" and ended with a march by Elgar. Attended by several classical music celebrities (Toscanini, Heifetz, Stravinsky), the concert made Gershwin the most talked about musician in America.

The success of *Rhapsody in Blue* paved the way for a spate of jazz-influenced classical works, and yet its own debt to jazz is largely superficial. Made up of one long movement (loosely divided into three sections: fast-slow-fast), *Rhapsody in Blue* is essentially a collection of jazz-inflected show tunes connected by the kind of virtuosic effects that are found in the piano concertos of Liszt or Tchaikovsky. The vivid orchestration was actually by Whiteman's arranger Ferde Grofé and the famous wailing clarinet glissando that opens the work so thrillingly was improvised in rehearsal by clarinettist Ross Gorman. None of which alters the fact that the Rhapsody still sounds incredibly fresh and exciting whether in Grofé's original arrangement or in his 1927 version for full orchestra.

Conductor Walter Damrosch was at the Whiteman concert and as a result Gershwin was commissioned to compose a "proper" piano concerto for the New York Symphony Orchestra. In fact though there is greater thematic development and the work is divided into clear-cut movements, the mixture is very much as before – a combination of a grand Romantic-style concerto and Dixieland rhythms, coloured by the melancholy tinge of both the blues and Yiddish popular music.

There's no piano in Gershwin's third orchestral work, which was largely inspired by two trips that he made to Paris: "My purpose here is to portray the impressions of an American visitor in Paris as he strolls about the city, listens to the various street noises, and absorbs the French atmosphere." It is thus a kind of easygoing tone poem, unspecific in its references though Gershwin did purchase some genuine French car horns to add to its authentically urban feel. There's a much more assured sense of structure than in his previous orchestral works, with less of a stop-start feel to it. Gershwin thought of it as a "rhapsodic ballet" and its combination of wide-eyed innocence and brash boulevardier spirit were perfectly captured by Gene Kelly's choreography in the 1951 film inspired by the piece.

In these three works – the sum of Gershwin's concert music – both orchestra and soloist need to shake off their inhibitions and embrace a more flexible "popular" idiom without becoming brash and unsubtle. André Previn is the ideal interpreter: his rapport with the orchestra is total and his own experiences as a jazz pianist mean that the Gershwin style comes easily to him. With a touch that is light and springy, he never over-indulges in the more sentimental passages and consistently taps into the humour that eludes many performers. Similarly in *An American in Paris* Previn directs a bustling performance which brings out all the work's bright cartoon colours and jauntiness with just enough hint of sleaze.

37

Edvard Grieg

Peer Gynt

Ilse Hollweg (soprano); Beecham Choral Society; Royal Philharmonic
Orchestra; Thomas Beecham (conductor)

EMI CDM5 66914 2; mid-price

Like film music, most incidental
music written for plays has proved
to be ephemeral, regardless of its
quality – Beethoven's music to
Goethe's *Egmont*, for example,
must be the least well-known of all
great compositions. Mendelssohn's
A Midsummer Night's Dream music
has fared rather better, as has
Grieg's music for Ibsen's *Peer Gynt*,
which did much to establish the
composer's reputation outside his native Norway.

Henrik Ibsen wrote his verse drama in 1867 but only decided
to adapt it for performance seven years later. He turned to Edvard
Grieg to provide the music and suggested – among other ideas –
that the whole of Act IV, depicting Peer's wanderings throughout
the world, be replaced by a "big musical tone painting." In the
end Grieg's music was rather more conventional in its ambitions,
ranging from songs and atmospheric passages to short sections to
cover scene changes. Grieg found the work a struggle, declaring
Peer Gynt "the most unmusical of all subjects." However, the first
production, in 1876, proved a huge success, and ran for 37 performances before a fire destroyed all the sets and costumes.

Dramatically *Peer Gynt* is a strange work: its combination of
folkloric detail and epic sweep is given a decidely modern twist
by the cynicism and amorality of its unscrupulous protagonist.
Grieg hoped to suggest irony in the music but it's hard to find it.
On the whole it's a richly effusive brand of Romanticism,

passionate and lyrical in a manner that sometimes recalls Tchaikovsky but without the older composer's visceral emotionalism. There are plenty of extraordinary dramatic moments for Grieg to get his teeth into, beginning with the village wedding (at which Peer abducts the bride) where an oompah-pah jollity and sense of revelry is cleverly undermined by more sinister tones. More famous is the nightmarish "In the Hall of the Mountain King", where Grieg suggests the mounting fury of the Trolls through a simple phrase that is repeated over and over in an increasingly frenzied manner. Yet more celebrated is "Morning" – beloved of TV advertisers – in which a fresh and radiant melody is passed between flute and oboe until it reaches a climax that for Grieg denoted "the sun breaking through the clouds."

On the whole, though, the dark moments outnumber the lighter ones, and the three women whom Peer abandons all have music of deep sadness, beginning with the richly sonorous "Ingrid's Lament" which bears some resemblance to the slow movement of Beethoven's *Symphony No. 7*. More funereal still is the solemn music that accompanies the death of Peer's mother Åse, its repeated three-note motif suggesting a life slowly ebbing away. Solveig, the woman who remains true to Peer, is represented by two highly emotional pieces: the first, "Solveig's Song", creates a wonderful sense of fragility with each of its lines seeming to peter out, while "Solveig's Lullaby" is more affirmative, its gentle melody, accompanied by tremolo high strings and harp, remaining just on the right side of sentimentality.

To give his music a life outside of Ibsen's drama, Grieg extracted two orchestral suites of four pieces each. On this recording, Sir Thomas Beecham conducts his own selection, comprising the eight pieces from the two suites plus the "Wedding March" and "Solveig's Lullaby". He also restores the chorus, and reinstates a soprano, Ilse Hollweg, for Solveig's two songs. Beecham was a conductor with a sure theatrical instinct and a great enthusiasm for Grieg, and few accounts of the *Peer Gynt* music are as fresh and vivid as his. Grieg's music can easily sound trite in the wrong hands, but Beecham's high-octane performance maximizes the excitement.

38

George Frideric Handel

Concerti grossi, Op. 6 Nos. 1–12

The Academy of Ancient Music; Andrew Manze (director)

Harmonia Mundi HMU 907228.89; 2 CDs; full price

The concerto grosso was a form of orchestral music that developed in the second half of the seventeenth century, with Corelli as its first great exponent. Like much instrumental music of the time, it consisted of a series of contrasting quick/slow movements based on dance forms. What was new about it was the division of the orchestra into two separate groups: a small ensemble of solo instruments, called the *concertino*, was set against a larger combination called the concerto grosso or *ripieno*. The groups played in alternation, with the larger group generally echoing the material of the smaller and creating a contrast between loud and soft passages.

Corelli's concertos remained hugely popular well into the eighteenth century, especially in England. But what spurred Handel to turn to the genre was the great success of two sets written by another Italian, the violinist Francesco Geminiani, a major London rival in the field of instrumental music. The six concertos of Handel's Opus 3 were published in 1734, with the twelve concertos of Opus 6 following in 1740. Both sets had a dual function: they could be used as interval music during performances of Handel's operas and oratorios, or as independently published pieces they could compete with the work of his Italian competitors. Together Handel's two sets constitute the final grand flourish of the concerto grosso form. Solo concertos, consisting of a more obvious "dialogue" between an individual soloist and the orchestra, were already proving more popular.

Apart from Bach's *Brandenburg Concertos* (see p.5), Handel's Opus 6 surpasses all other concerti grossi in scope and ambition. Scored for strings alone (though he later added oboes), these concertos are much more expansive than those of Corelli, there's more contrast between the movements, and themes are developed in a far more imaginative way. Many of the second movements are fugal, and there are several sections for the soloists to demonstrate their prowess, like the last movement of *No. 11*. The last of the twelve concertos to be completed (all were written at incredible speed in October 1739), *No. 11* is the liveliest of them all, with a marvellous opening Andante in which a stately theme is wittily undercut through a phrase of repeated notes that double in speed at the start of each bar. The very last concerto, *No. 12* in B minor, forms a suitable climax: bristling with restless energy and yet full of mystery, its has in its central movement a characteristically serene Handel melody (hard not to imagine it being sung) that is twice repeated in variation form.

The Academy of Ancient Music is one of the world's leading "authentic" ensembles, that is to say they use instruments of the same period as the music and observe Baroque performance conventions. With a string orchestra playing Baroque music this means smaller forces than was previously customary, gut strings and an absence of vibrato. This produces a slightly raw and upfront sound when compared to an entirely "modern" performance and is not to everyone's taste. The brio and authority with which the Academy approaches this music, however, is enough to convince any sceptic. Andrew Manze directs the ensemble from his position of leader of the orchestra (first violin) with a good deal of verve and energy. His generally fleet-footed and light approach brings out the mercurial brilliance of these concertos, but the sound is always rich and refined, and those essential Handelian elements of formal swagger, graceful melodiousnes and sheer ebullience are communicated with great vividness.

39

George Frideric Handel

Water Music; Music for the Royal Fireworks

Le Concert des Nations; Jordi Savall (conductor)

Auvidis Fontanalis ES 8512; full price

On July 17, 1717, King George I and his entourage enjoyed a lavish trip down the Thames from Lambeth to Chelsea, which the Daily Courant described as follows: "Many barges with Persons of Quality attended, and so great a Number of Boats, that the whole River in a manner was cover'd; a City Company's Barge was employ'd for the Musick, wherein were 50 Instruments of all sorts, who play'd . . . the finest Symphonies, compos'd express for this Occasion, by Mr Hendel; which his Majesty liked so well, that he caus'd it to be plaid three times in going and returning."

What the Courant called "Symphonies" were actually a group of orchestral suites which collectively became known as the *Water Music*. The orchestral suite, which had developed in Germany in emulation of the formal elegance of French court music, consisted of a set of contrasting dances modelled on those found in the operas and ballets of Lully – Louis XIV's principal composer. To French elegance Handel added some English rumbustiousness in the form of hornpipes and country dances.

No autograph score exists of the *Water Music*, so the order of the dances is a matter of guesswork. What is generally agreed is that there are three distinct suites, in different keys, for various combinations of instruments. Each suite has its own particular character. The F major is the most radiant and the most grandiloquent: scored for two oboes, bassoon, two horns and strings, it's the first use of Baroque horns in English music and they dominate the set even though they're not used in every movement. The five-movement D major suite adds two trumpets and kettledrums to the band and the result is much more martial in tone. On this recording movements from this suite are combined with the most intimate of the suites, the one in G which was probably played as the royal party dined at Lord Ranelagh's villa at Chelsea. Its mixture of recorder, flute and strings has a much more "indoor" feel to it, as does the delicate sprightliness of its French-style dances.

Thirty-one years later Handel wrote another grand ceremonial suite, to commemorate the end of the War of the Austrian Succession. The music was to accompany a spectacular firework display held in Green Park, London which, in the event, proved rather a disaster – Catherine wheels failed to ignite, a pavilion caught fire, and the designer of the spectacle, Servandoni, drew his sword on the man in charge of the fireworks. King George II insisted that any music be played on war-like instruments with no "fidles" (sic). Handel eventually agreed and scored the work for a battery of oboes, bassoons, horns, trumpets and drums (but later added strings for future concert performances). The result is a work of great pomp and a large element of triumphalism, especially in the long overture. *The Music for the Royal Fireworks* is much more of an "occasional" work than the *Water Music*, neither as subtle nor as ingratiating but still extremely enjoyable.

Handel's ceremonial music really benefits from being played on period instruments, and its mainly outdoor character needs a vigorous and energetic approach – which it certainly gets from Jordi Savall and Le Concert des Nations. There is none of the politeness and emphasis on a clean sound at all costs that you get with some period orchestras. This is an outfit that does not shy away from the more gutsy and lurid colours that their instruments are capable of producing. In the *Water Music* the brass playing is particularly raw and powerful, and overall there is an abiding sense of this music being written to uplift and entertain.

40

George Frideric Handel

Messiah

Joan Rodgers (soprano), Della Jones (mezzo-soprano), Christopher Robson (counter-tenor), Philip Langridge (tenor), Bryn Terfel (bass-baritone); Collegium Musicum 90; Richard Hickox (conductor)

Chandos CHAN 0522/3; 2 CDs; full price

The oratorio – the musical dramatization of a religious text – emerged in Italy at the end of the sixteenth century at the same time as its secular equivalent, opera. Indeed, any composer who worked in one genre tended to work in both. In England, oratorios were largely unknown until George Frideric Handel fashioned his own version in a manner calculated to appeal to middle-class Protestant taste. Like their Italian equivalents, most of Handel's oratorios used stories from the Bible, but what made them different, in addition to the fact that they were sung in English, was the prevalence of choruses, a feature that drew on the rich tradition of the English anthem. In Handel's day oratorios were performed in concert halls or theatres rather than churches, but they were not operas – although the narrative of many of them makes staging perfectly feasible.

Messiah, by far and away the most celebrated of Handel's oratorios, is actually the least typical because it doesn't tell a story. Handel's librettist was a previous collaborator, the evangelical clergyman and scholar Charles Jennens, whose skilful collage of biblical excerpts was intended to create a presentation of Christ as the world's saviour, in which the dominant mood was one of contemplation – an intention partly countered by the sheer exuberance of much of Handel's music. Handel wrote the work at his usual lightning rate (less than a month), and the first performance took place in Dublin on April 13, 1742, with the profits being distributed between two hospitals and a debtors' prison. Such was the demand for tickets that the organizers, to make more room, requested ladies not to wear hooped dresses and men not to carry swords.

Messiah has remained enormously popular ever since, and not just in Protestant countries – in Catholic Austria, a re-orchestrated version was commissioned from Mozart. Much of its appeal lies in the simple directness with which Handel expresses his religious convictions. The wealth of beautiful arias vary greatly in both type and mood – from the grandiose "He was despised" to the simple, touching lyricism of "How beautiful are the feet" and the clamorous declamation of "The trumpet shall sound". What they all have in common is a clarity of feeling and an unfussiness that is instantly enjoyable. Handel was a commercially astute artist, and he meant *Messiah* to be entertaining as well as uplifting. Hence the magnificent choruses in which grand ceremonial music is frequently combined with elaborate counterpoint, creating something that seems almost to be inviting the audience to join in – the "Hallelujah Chorus" being the most famous example. By the closing chorus "Worthy is the Lamb" and the magnificent fugal "Amen", there's an overwhelming sense of contentment and spiritual well-being that is in marked distinction to the final anguished solemnity of Bach's *St Matthew Passion* (see p.8).

There are a great number of *Messiah* recordings in the catalogue but very few of them are entirely satisfactory, largely because the relatively simple solo parts need four or five well-matched and expressive singers capable of communicating the power of the words. This recording hits the mark in that respect, with a fine group of soloists – all seasoned opera singers – who really sound as though they mean what they are singing. Particularly outstanding are Bryn Terfel and Philip Langridge, whose first recitative, "Comfort ye", immediately establishes the right mood of fervent expectation. Richard Hickox's conducting conjures up the sense of occasion that is so vital for this work, and all the most spine-tingling moments forcefully succeed in hitting the target.

41

Joseph Haydn

String Quartets Op. 76, Nos. 1–3

Kodály Quartet

Naxos 8.550314; budget price

The string quartet combines four instruments – two violins, a viola and a cello – that are capable of producing very similar sounds as well as subtly distinct ones. The genre was more or less invented by Joseph Haydn in the 1750s, probably to provide outdoor music that didn't require any instruments that weren't easy to carry around. From such relatively modest beginnings, Haydn developed the quartet over a forty-year period into a form that Goethe was memorably to compare to "a stimulating conversation between four intelligent people". Haydn's example prompted his friend Mozart (with whom he played quartets) into writing his own, and both men's work in the genre stimulated Beethoven to push the quartet into ever more expressive territory.

The most famous Haydn quartets are the six of Op. 76, which mark the culmination of his quest for expressive perfection. Commissioned by a Viennese nobleman called Count Joseph Erdödy, they were completed in 1797 when Haydn had turned 65. He must have felt some satisfaction with the outcome, for they are the strongest and most finely wrought of all his chamber compositions and inspired his pupil Beethoven's first attempts at quartet writing – even if he was reluctant to admit the influence.

In the first three quartets of Op. 76 set you can find everything with which Haydn's style is synonymous: ingenious variation, complex fugal writing, folk-influenced melodies, brilliant ensemble writing and general transparency. All the quartets are in four movements and the range of expression is astonishingly wide. The opening movement of *No. 1* prefigures the forcefulness of Beethoven in its sudden fortissimo outbursts. *No. 2*, nicknamed the *"Fifths"* because of the interval of its opening phrase, uses the contrast between major and minor keys to create a mood of tension especially in its first and last movements. Its so-called "Witches' Minuet" is a fine example of Haydn letting his hair down with a lively canon – the violins play together in octaves, while the lower instruments do the same, but one bar behind.

Best of all is No. 3 in C major, known as *"The Emperor"* on account of its slow movement, a beautiful set of unostentatious variations on a hymn-like theme composed in response to England's national anthem and later adopted as the Austrian one. It shows how far the quartet has developed in the way each of the four instruments gets an equal share of the spotlight. The preceding Allegro is one of Haydn's most spirited exercises in counterpoint, further enlivened when the main theme returns with a syncopated drone bass to give it a rustic and distinctly central European flavour. The short and chirpy Minuet and Trio is followed by a hard-driven finale heralded by a motif of three harsh chords which punctuate the movement at regular intervals.

The Kodály Quartet from Hungary have recorded a complete cycle of Haydn's quartets for the budget label Naxos. Their readings of the first three Op. 76 quartets possess a steady, reliable elegance that's typical of their approach to the entire cycle. They are expressive without sentimentalizing the often lush writing, and there's a liveliness to their playing that makes the music sound freshly minted. Slow movements are often quite leisurely but there is never any sense of indulgence: rather there's a feeling that they want to present the music in as pristinely classical a manner as possible. The somewhat recessed sound contributes to a slightly distant sensation that is nonetheless completely appropriate. The spectacularly low price is an added attraction.

42

Joseph Haydn

Symphonies Nos. 96, 103 & 104

Royal Concertgebouw Orchestra; Colin Davis (conductor)

Philips 446 576-2; budget price

Most of Haydn's 104 symphonies were written for the aristocratic Esterházy family, his employers for nearly thirty years. But when, in 1790, Prince Nikolaus Esterházy died, Haydn became, effectively, a free agent. Soon after, he received an offer from the impresario J.P. Salomon – who also approached Mozart – to write six symphonies for a series of public concerts in London. In the event Haydn made two visits to London and wrote twelve symphonies (though not in the order which they are numbered). The *"London" Symphonies* (Nos. 93–104) were hugely successful and are his greatest achievement in the genre. All follow the four-movement pattern of Haydn's maturity, but the orchestra is larger than ever before, and the harmonies more daring, with frequent unexpected moves to different keys.

Symphony No. 96 in D, the first of the sequence to be performed, shows Haydn at his most good-humoured and sophisticated, very much aiming to entertain. The outer movements are jaunty and vivacious and Haydn specified that the short finale be played as fast as possible. This is a symphony with few dark corners; there's a brief flurry of ominous-sounding counterpoint in the middle of the slow movement and some dramatic interjections in the last, but that's all. What stands out is the imaginative orchestration – a beautiful cadenza for two violins at the end of the first movement and some exquisite woodwind and brass touches in the Andante's first theme.

The very first bar of *Symphony No. 103* – a drum-roll – is a marvellous, unprecedented coup, which inevitably led to the symphony's becoming known as the "*Drum Roll*". This dramatic flourish announces one of Haydn's most original works, leading into a quiet, sustained phrase for bassoons, cellos and basses which has a mystery comparable to the opening of Schubert's "*Unfinished*" *Symphony*. Later in the symphony there's a masterful set of double variations on two themes derived from folk tunes, a Trio that makes intriguing use of the clarinets, and a finale that is ingeniously based upon a single theme.

With *Symphony No. 104* Haydn takes his leave of the genre with a work of exquisite refinement. A slow funereal introduction leads to what seems to be the lightest and most lyrical of Allegros but which gets increasingly resolute and dramatic the more it progresses. As in *No. 96*, the Andante contrasts its dignified outer sections with a moment of explosive gloom at its centre. One of Haydn's wittiest Minuets then follows, complete with unexpected drum-rolls and sudden silences. Legend has it that the melody over a drone bass that dominates the last movement was inspired by the London street cry "Hot cross buns". Its more likely source is the Slavonic dance music which Haydn frequently turned to and indeed the tune bears a marked resemblance to Smetana's *Czech Dance No. 8*, written some seventy years later.

That Haydn's "*London*" *Symphonies* sound as bright and zestful when given the big symphony orchestra treatment as they do when played by smaller and more "authentic" ensembles is borne out by these outstanding performances, made in the late 1970s and early 1980s. The vigour and freshness of the Concertgebouw's playing is due, in no small measure, to Colin Davis's energetic conducting: speeds tend to be broad but the sense of each movement's direction and shape is never lost sight of, while the deft touches of instrumental colouring (which is such a feature of these works) are exquisitely highlighted. Davis's occasional tendency to hum along is a barely discernible distraction.

43

Joseph Haydn

Missa in angustiis ("Nelson Mass"); Te Deum

Felicity Lott (soprano), Carolyn Watkinson (contralto), Maldwyn Davies
(tenor), David Wilson-Johnson (bass); The English Concert Choir and
Orchestra; Trevor Pinnock (conductor)

Archiv 423 097-2; full price

Haydn was a deeply religious man
and much of his most heartfelt and
passionate music can be found in
his sacred choral works.
Unfortunately his activities as a
composer for the church were cur-
tailed by an imperial edict of 1783
restricting the use of orchestral
music in the Catholic liturgy. The
one advantage of this was that,
when the ban was lifted, Haydn
returned to writing sacred music with a new-found confidence
that enabled him to produce works of a hitherto unknown power
and profundity. Supreme among these were the six final Masses
that he wrote, commissioned on a yearly basis by Prince Nikolaus
Esterházy for his wife's name day, the most exciting of which is the
Missa in angustiis, popularly known as the "Nelson Mass". Haydn
wrote the third of his last set of Masses in the summer of 1798,
naming it *Missa in angustiis* – Mass in anxious times. The anxiety
was caused by Napoleon Bonaparte, who had shelled Vienna the
year before and was now campaigning in Egypt. Its more common
title was bestowed in honour of the British admiral who destroyed
the French fleet in August 1798, and for whom the Mass was performed two years later when he visited the Esterházys at Eisenstadt.

With an orchestra of three trumpets, timpani, strings and
organ (the prince had disbanded the wind players), it begins
with a nerve-racked and edgy Kyrie in which the soprano

soloist's brilliant runs soar above the chorus in the most thrilling manner imaginable. Unusually this section (along with a sombre setting of the Benedictus) is in D minor, while the rest of the mass is more celebratory – although the restless energy of the opening never seems far away.

One of the glories of Haydn's late Masses is the way choruses, solos and ensemble passages are so seamlessly integrated – each section seeming to grow out of the previous one. This is especially evident in the two longest sections, the Gloria and the Credo, both of which have a symphonic three-movement structure. The Gloria abounds with many wonderful touches: the joyous question–and–answer exhanges between solo and chorus at the beginning, the penitential sobriety of its middle section, the cascading flow of its fugal conclusion. Throughout the Mass there's a constant shifting between major and minor keys which gives it a particularly dramatic quality. This is most strikingly evident in the Benedictus, conventionally a section of serene optimism, but here treated as something darkly ominous.

For a performance of the *Nelson Mass* to succeed, it's absolutely essential that the opening Kyrie has just the right degree of tension plus a soprano capable of soaring above the chorus with spine-tingling ease. This recording gets there with room to spare: Felicity Lott has just the right kind of operatic panache but is never exaggerated, and her voice combines beautifully with the other three soloists. This was a pioneeringly "authentic" account when it appeared in 1987, and it still sounds extremely vivid with the slightly drier tone of the instruments and the relatively small chorus helping to reinforce both the crucial sense of unease and the many moments of joyous excitement. In addition, this CD features a fine version of the short but splendid *Te Deum* that was also performed as part of the celebrations that welcomed Nelson to Eisenstadt. Written for chorus only with no solo sections, it's a generally bright and optimistic work, divided into three sections (fast, slow, fast) of which the central one provides a brief moment of solemnity.

44

Hildegard of Bingen

Canticles of Ecstasy

Sequentia; Barbara Thornton (director)

Deutsche Harmonia Mundi 05472 77320; full price

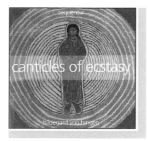

Twenty years ago Hildegard of Bingen (1098–1179) was unknown to all but the most erudite of medievalists. Today she is something of a cult figure, whose extraordinarily wide-ranging gifts – as scholar and mystic as well as a composer – appeal to feminists, academics and New-Agers alike. This explosion of interest is almost entirely due to a recording made in 1981 by the early music group Gothic Voices (see p.98), which unexpectedly became a bestseller. The passionate intensity of Hildegard's music came as something of a shock, especially since it is entirely monophonic – just a single line of melody with no supporting harmony.

Like many daughters of the nobility, Hildegard was sent to a monastic institution at an early age, living in seclusion (in a walled-up cell) with the anchoress Jutta at the Benedictine monastery of Disibodenberg in southern Germany. When Jutta died in 1136, Hildegard took over the leadership of the small group of nuns attached to the monastery. Five years later she began to experience a series of visions which were dictated and recorded in a book titled *Scivias* (Know the Ways). The language of these visions, and of the religious poetry that she set to her own music, is highly personal and full of startling images, both apocalyptic and sensual – "When I was forty-two years and seven months old, the heavens were opened and a blinding light of exceptional brilliance flowed through my entire brain. And so it kindled my whole heart and breast like a flame, not burning but warming."

A few years after these visions began, against the wishes of her abbot, Hildegard left the monastery with eighteen nuns and her secretary – a monk named Volmar – to found an independent community on the Rupertsberg, near Bingen. It was here, in the 1150s, that she gathered together her liturgical songs into a collection which she called *Symphonia harmoniae, caelestium revalationum* (Symphony of the harmony of heavenly revelations). The word "Symphonia" signified for her not just the harmonious combination of various musical sounds but also the divine harmony of the cosmos, and she saw the act of making music as a union between the physical and the spiritual that brought the participant closer to the divine. Hildegard's musical language has the same inspired quality as her poetry. It is not based on the traditional formulas of plainchant but consists of freely composed melodic lines with rich embellishments and frequent leaps that, in performance, convey an intensely rapturous and ethereal quality.

Of the many Hildegard recordings that have appeared since 1981, the finest are those by the group Sequentia, who have now recorded every surviving note of the music that she composed. *Canticles of Ecstasy* is a collection of fifteen songs dedicated to either the Virgin Mary or the Holy Spirit. Hildegard's melodies tend to conform to a similar pattern but, even so, there are subtle changes of mood between pieces which range from the soaring fluidity of *O vis aeternatis* to the more modest and grounded *Quia ergo femina*. Sequentia's director, the late Barbara Thornton, varies the music further by the occasional, discreet addition of instruments (fiddles and a harp) and by dividing the songs within her all-female choir, with frequent alternations between solo and ensemble singing. All the singers have a clear, unforced tone but the individuality of each voice shines through the resonant acoustic of the church of St Pantaleon in Cologne, even in ensemble passages. The result is a near-perfect balance between ecstatic conviction and inner serenity.

45

Charles Ives

Three Places in New England; Symphony No. 3

Saint Louis Symphony Orchestra; Leonard Slatkin (conductor)

RCA 09026-61222-2; full price

Composers of classical music in nineteenth-century America tended to look to Europe for their training and their musical inspiration. Few were concerned to find a specifically American voice, and they virtually ignored the indigenous and popular music that thrived around them. Charles Ives, who was born in 1874, was one of the exceptions: the son of a small-town band leader, Ives studied music at Yale and went on to compose music that bears traces of hymn tunes, band music, spirituals, Stephen Foster songs and much else, all melded into a coherent (or sometimes not so coherent) whole. Ives was also an experimenter, as pioneering in his way as his exact contemporary Schoenberg. He regularly employed polytonality (the use of different keys simultaneously), dissonance and quarter tones, at a time when such innovations were totally unacceptable to the concert-going public – indeed, it's only since the centenary of his birth in 1974 that performances of Ives have become commonplace. Realizing the unlikelihood of making a living as a composer, Ives worked (extremely successfully) in the insurance business and wrote music in his spare time.

Nearly all of Ives's music was inspired by aspects of American life – in particular, by memories of his New England childhood. His *Symphony No. 3*, written between 1901 and 1904 and subtitled "The Camp Meeting", evokes the atmosphere of an outdoor religious gathering using favourite hymns like "What a

Friend We Have in Jesus" and "Just As I Am Without One Plea" to build the outer movements' melodic and harmonic structures. He makes the middle movement the fast one, a jaunty Allegro whose energy seems to derive from individual strands of counterpoint that have a will and a direction of their own.

Ives's concern with simultaneity, his desire to convey all the myriad sounds that might bombard a person at any one time, is most vividly expressed in one of his finest works, *Three Places in New England* (1903–14). Each movement attempts to capture a specific sense of place and all its rich associations. "The 'St Gaudens' in Boston Common" refers to a statue of Colonel Shaw, who led a regiment of black soldiers during the Civil War. The slow unfolding of misty, heavy chords suggests something dreamlike and ghostly. Gradually little snippets of clarity emerge and the vaguest hint – like a memory – of the tune "Marching Through Georgia" can just be made out. The second movement, "Putnam's Camp", is a thrilling, toe-tapping mélange of military band music briefly interrupted by a diaphanous, floating chord. It was inspired by a childhood memory of Ives's father arranging for two bands to march across a park from different directions while playing completely different music. "The Housatonic at Stockbridge", suggested by a Sunday morning walk, is Ives at his most transcendent and visionary: a burble of strings and a gradually emerging hymn tune create a mood of tranquil serenity that builds to an ecstatic climax before suddenly dying away.

Leonard Slatkin and his orchestra meet the challenge of Ives's often rumbustious style head on: rather than iron out the rough edges and the idiosyncrasies, they celebrate them in such a way that the logic of Ives's musical vision seems perfectly clear. *Three Places in New England* comes over as a vigorously original masterpiece, its three quite different moods captured with great sensitivity. *The Symphony No. 3* (a score which Mahler came close to conducting) sounds no less visionary in Slatkin's detailed interpretation. As well as these two works, this disc also contains the mysterious *The Unanswered Question* and a second orchestral essay, *Central Park in the Dark*.

46

Leoš Janáček

String Quartets No. 1 ("Kreutzer Sonata") & No. 2 ("Intimate Pages")

Talich Quartet

Supraphon 11 1354 2; full price

Like many central European composers of his time, Janáček was fascinated by the indigenous cultural traditions of his homeland, and in 1888 he set off to explore his native Moravia with the ethnographer František Bartoš. The visit proved the catalyst in the formation of a personal style: in particular, the inflections of Moravian speech patterns and the short, irregular phrases of Moravian folk music became integral to his musical language. But an even greater inspiration occurred in 1917 when Janáček met Kamila Stösslová, a married woman half his age. During the last ten years of his life, Janáček's all-consuming passion for Kamila prompted an astonishing creative renewal that was to produce his greatest and most emotionally charged music.

The most overt expression of Janáček's infatuation with Kamila is in the two string quartets. The first, written in 1921, is known as the "*Kreutzer Sonata*" after Tolstoy's novella of that name, in which a performance of Beethoven's *Kreutzer Sonata* forms the key moment in a tale of jealousy and murder. The quartet never corresponds precisely to the story – instead Janáček transforms Tolstoy's cautionary tale into a display of extreme emotions. The music is fragmentated and has a rawness that is unnervingly direct. In the second movement a jaunty melody is suddenly interrupted by a tremolando motif which seems to presage some terrible disaster. A version of a lyrical theme from Beethoven's sonata makes a brief appearance in the third movement of the quartet, but even this terminates in a squall of demi-semiquavers as if to suggest the transience of human happiness. Only in the closing bars is there a slight hint of release and reconciliation.

The second quartet is only marginally more restrained. Written in 1928, the last year of Janáček's life, each of its four movements was intended as a love letter to Kamila. "It's a work as if carved out of living flesh," he wrote. "I think that I won't write a more profound and a truer one." As in the first quartet, there's an abundance of short-breathed angular phrases and obsessive repetitions that seem to signify sudden changes of mood. This volatility is particularly evident in the outer movements and it's hard not to relate it to frustration and ambivalence on Janáček's part. The relationship was never a reciprocal one and Kamila tended to humour the old man rather than return his affection. Repeatedly music that is warmly passionate is followed by something cold, as in the opening passage where a boldly passionate statement is answered by the ghostly sound of the viola playing as close to the bridge as possible. Even the mournful lullaby that forms the third movement has an anxious edge to its second half, while the manic finale seems like a stream-of-consciousness in which delight and hysteria are virtually indistinguishable.

The Talich Quartet bring out the neuroticism of these works in performances that are vigorous and hard-driven, although never to the point of producing an ugly sound. They are particularly good at making the sudden switches of mood seem genuinely alarming without resorting to melodrama. The recording is quite forward sounding, which, combined with the quartet's bold attack and often intense vibrato, makes for a suitably oppressive and claustrophobic atmosphere. As if to compensate for the unrelenting emotional pressure of the two quartets, the disc also includes the four-movement wind sextet *Mládí* (Youth); it's another late work, but this one has an infectious liveliness that's just occasionally coloured by moments of melancholy.

47

György Ligeti

Works for piano: Études; Musica ricercata

Pierre-Laurent Aimard (piano)

Sony SK 62308; full price

Of all the leading figures of the post-war avant-garde, the Hungarian composer György Ligeti has always been receptive to the widest range of influences and ideas – from fractal geometry and the visual conundrums of M.C. Escher to the music of Central Africa and the jazz piano of Thelonious Monk. Two elements, however, frequently recur in his work: a fascination with polyrhythm – the simultaneous use of two or more rhythms in different lines of music – and a wry (and often dark) sense of humour.

Ligeti has written piano music intermittently throughout his career. His first significant piece for the instrument, *Musica ricercata*, was composed when he was still a lecturer at the Music Academy in Budapest. The archaic title literally means "researched" or "learned" music, and in these eleven pieces Ligeti pays homage to and expands upon tradition. For a Hungarian composer the example of Bartók is never far away, and his legacy is clearly present in the percussive energy of several pieces. There's also a certain element of "back to basics" on display here: the first piece uses notes of just one pitch (until the very last note); the second is constructed from a repertoire of two pitches; the third from three, and so on. The variety of moods that Ligeti creates through this self-imposed discipline is startling: the sixth piece, a witty conflation of jazz and Baroque, is followed by a lurching and melancholy waltz, but the most exciting moments are provided by the seventh, in which a pulsating, hypnotic ostinato (shades of Reich ten years before his time) is overlaid with a wistful lyrical melody in a completely different metre.

This combination of rhythmic adventurousness and expressivity re-surfaces thirty years later with the start of a series of *Piano Études* in 1985. Ligeti claims to have been drawn to the idea of writing virtuosic piano pieces because his own inability as a player prevented him fully realizing his love for the instrument. Certainly they are very difficult works, with an emphasis on building up conflicting layers of tempo. But there's a greater sensuousness on display, and Ligeti has claimed that in writing for piano "tactile concepts are almost as important as acoustic ones . . . A well-formed piano work produces physical pleasure." In several pieces Ligeti creates a shimmering haze of pianistic colours that often seems indebted to the Debussy of the *Images* and *Children's Corner* (see p.53). This tendency is at its most poetic in the sixth étude, *Automne à Varsovie*, in which as many as four overlapping lines create an impression of swirling mists which eventually builds to a climactic whirlwind of sound. But, as in *Musica ricercata*, it's Ligeti's synthesizing eclecticism that is so dazzling: from the cool beauty of the Satiesque *Arc-en-ciel*, through the fluttering, chromaticism of *Vértige* and the ricocheting pseudo-gamelan of *Galamb borong* – these pieces testify to Ligeti's ability to find in the piano an almost limitless number of possibilities.

Ligeti's *Piano Études* have proved an exciting challenge to pianists, and there is a surprising number of recordings available. This disc, part of an ongoing project by Sony to record all Ligeti's music, is undoubtedly the best. Pierre-Laurent Aimard manages the technical difficulties of Ligeti's polyrhythmic approach with complete assurance. More importantly, he seems to inhabit these works so thoroughly as to be able to bring out a kaleidoscopic array of nuances and gradations of colour. One moment he's making the piano sound like a battery of demented xylophones, the next he's overlapping the most exquisite veils of sounds. It's an exceptional performance.

48

Franz Liszt

Sonata in B minor and other pieces

Krystian Zimerman (piano)

Deutsche Grammophon 431 780-2; full price

In certain circles Franz Liszt is not taken altogether seriously, and the reason for this lies in his flamboyant brilliance as a pianist. Liszt, the argument goes, was all self-promotion and no substance; his formidable technique forced him to create music that would do justice to it, and many of his works are simply vehicles for keyboard wizardry. On top of this, his long hair and saturnine good looks created an image of demonic genius that proved irresistible to a number of women but less so to many critics. The critic Eduard Hanslick spoke for many when he claimed that Liszt's main role as a performer was "to fill the gap left by the absence of musical content or to justify the atrociousness of what content there is".

Out of a vast catalogue of solo piano music, only a handful of pieces are now performed with any regularity, and of these just one – the *Sonata in B minor* – is universally regarded as a masterpiece. Composed between 1851 and 1853, and dedicated to Schumann, it is cast (like Schumann's *Fantasie in C*) in three movements that are played without a pause. It's a vast work whose musical span is underlaid by a series of themes and motifs that grow, fuse and eventually expire. Three of the sonata's main motifs are stated in the opening bars: first a softly ominous descending phrase, followed by a wildly animated one, and third a low growl of repeated notes in the bass. Liszt weaves them together and drives them along in a whirl of furious semiquavers until an escalation of the first motif leads into a "big tune" of grandiose dimensions, which almost immediately disappears. The rest of the movement is a kaleidoscope of thematic transformations, one of which turns another of the initial motifs into a lyric melody of Chopinesque tenderness.

The second movement ushers in a mood of subdued solemnity, even of religiosity. A new tranquil theme is introduced which some of Liszt's pupils associated with the character of Gretchen in Goethe's *Faust*, though there is no evidence that Liszt intended a Faustian subtext for the sonata. According to this theory the finale represents a picture of Mephistopheles and it's certainly not difficult to project a demonic fury onto this Allegro marked (like the first movement) "energico". It begins with two of the original motifs treated as a brilliant and extremely manic fugue that builds into a phantasmagorical review of most of the previous themes. It's a *tour de force* of bravura virtuosity that in its most exhibitionist passages seems to anticipate Tchaikovsky. It ends – after a long dramatic pause – with a coda of quiet reflection.

From the opening notes of Krystian Zimerman's meteoric performance, it is clear that he really believes in the sonata's greatness. Too many interpreters treat it either as a barnstorming melodrama that will reveal their own virtuosity, or as the rather unwieldy successor to Beethoven's late sonatas. In Zimerman's hands it's the sonata's visionary dimension that stands out: it feels as if every phrase has been carefully thought out in terms of weight and colour so that the work's undoubted histrionic quality is tempered by moments of iridescent delicacy and inner calm. Of the four shorter pieces included on the disc the most remarkable are the two late works, *Nuages Gris* (1881) and *La lugubre gondola II* (1882). Liszt in old age developed an austere, inward-looking style which in its economy, emphasis on atmosphere and ambiguous tonality seems, in these sensitive performances, like an uncanny presentiment of the piano music of Debussy.

49

Guillaume de Machaut

The Mirror of Narcissus

Gothic Voices with Emma Kirkby; Christopher Page (director)

Hyperion CDA 66087; full price

Guillaume de Machaut (c.1300–1377) was one of the greatest and most original of all medieval composers, and even today his music often sounds strikingly modern, with its leaping melodies and startling clashes of notes. He wrote in a new style, known as the Ars Nova, that exploited a number of recent technical innovations in music, most notably a fixed rhythmic pattern of great complexity called isorhythm, but Machaut also employed more old-fashioned (indeed, declining) musical forms, and many of his most touching songs are simple, single-voiced works.

Machaut was revered by his contemporaries as much for his prowess as a poet as for his musical skill (Geoffrey Chaucer was a great admirer), and much of his life was spent in the service of a succession of aristocratic patrons, including King John of Bohemia and Charles of Navarre, the future King of France. The music of the courts was primarily concerned with love, and nearly all Machaut's compositions are love songs, despite the fact that he held several honorary positions in the church. Such songs conformed to fairly rigid formal constraints. They dealt with the rarefied world of courtly love, where the object of desire is an unattainable woman of unrivalled beauty whose admirer swears undying devotion to her even though she is the cause of as much pain as pleasure. Machaut's poetic language is very much in the tradition of the Troubadours of northern France, those itinerant singer-songwriters who performed their work at the chateaux of the nobility, and to a large extent his songs were the pop music of their day, albeit for a highly exclusive clientele.

The more traditional aspect of Machaut's work finds expression in his most favoured song form, the already slightly outmoded *virelai* for solo voice, in which a refrain is alternated with three stanzas. In contrast, Machaut's polyphonic songs (*ballades and rondeaux*) are far more adventurous and possess greater rhythmic variety, often using a form of syncopation called the hocket (from the Latin for hiccup), which breaks up the line of a melody in one voice by inserting sudden gaps which are often filled by the other voices, thus creating a gentle undulating quality.

Gothic Voices are an outstanding English group, employing both male and female singers, who specialize in music of the Middle Ages. The group's director, Christopher Page, prefers to perform the songs *a cappella* (with voices only); a valid alternative would have been to have instruments doubling the lower parts. The decision is fully justified by the wonderful textual clarity that results. Unaccompanied performances of the polyphonic songs show off their complexity in a highly immediate way. The disc opens with a dazzling *ballade* titled *Dame, de qui toute ma joie vient*, which sways and pulsates with an extraordinary energy while at the same time exuding an underlying melancholy. There's a much stronger sense than in later polyphony of the independence of the four voices, as if the fact that they combine so beautifully is largely incidental. This is even more marked in the one sacred work on the disc, the motet *Inviolata genitrix*, where it really does sound, at moments, as if three people were singing completely different songs simultaneously.

The disc alternates the polyphonic songs with the simpler *virelais* — six in total — and shares them between five singers. The subject matter if not the form of these songs is the same but they possess all the clear directness and memorability of folk song; it's a style that is particularly suited to the pure, unaffected tones of soprano Emma Kirkby who performs two of them.

50

Gustav Mahler

Symphony No. 5

Vienna Philharmonic; Leonard Bernstein (conductor)

Deutsche Grammophon 423 608-2; full price

"The symphony is the world! The symphony must embrace every thing." Gustav Mahler's struggle to fulfill his own dictum was one of the most compelling artistic enterprises of the last hundred years. Mahler conceived his nine completed symphonies on the grandest of scales but with a view of the world that was profoundly ambiguous. His obsession with death and permanent sense of social alienation was relieved only by a belief in the power of love and the transcendence of nature. His music reflects a personality pulled apart by anxiety and doubt: in a Mahler symphony the most disparate elements collide awkwardly with each other – tremulously ecstatic string writing next to abrasive military marches, the sounds of nature alongside banal popular melodies. The idiom may often seem Romantic, but its fragmentation and instability are profoundly modern.

The *Symphony No. 5* was written between 1901 and 1903, but Mahler continued to revise it until his death in 1911. Following a clear progression from a mood of dark despair to joyful reconciliation, its five movements are divided into three distinct parts. Part I begins with an unnerving minor key fanfare that seems to herald some dreadful tragedy. A funeral march of quiet desperation follows, periodically interrupted by passages of extreme emotional violence. The violence is intensified in the second movement, which is dominated by a demented restlessness interspersed with brief moments of calm. Part II consists entirely of one movement, a Scherzo, which in its initial guise of forceful jollity provides a shocking contrast to the preceding movements. All is not as it seems, however, and the exuberant triple-time dance rhythms are gradually transformed into something edgy and sinister.

The Adagietto that commences Part III was conceived as a love-poem for the beautiful Alma Schindler, a talented musician some twenty years Mahler's junior, whom he married in 1902. Made famous by its subsequent use in Visconti's film *Death in Venice*, its radiant combination of strings and harp provides a serene oasis at the heart of the work. And yet there's an underlying sadness to it, the frailty of the sound perhaps suggesting the ephemerality and fragility of life. The finale, which follows without a break, has no such vulnerability: an initially rustic feel is established via an exchange of wind instruments – horn calling to bassoon, clarinet and oboe. The movement builds in speed with a scurrying fugal passage that reveals Mahler's admiration for Bach. Textures become increasingly thick and complex but the overwhelming sensation is of an exuberant, pulsating energy which Mahler expert Deryck Cooke describes as an "artistic joy in symphonic creation, of building up a large musical structure". This sense of affirmation climaxes with a glorious chorale-like figure in the brass that is rapidly overwhelmed by an explosive flurry of a conclusion.

As a Jewish conductor-composer, Leonard Bernstein felt an intense identification with Mahler and he was one of his greatest modern interpreters. Sometimes his performances could come perilously close to kitsch, while at others he seemed to reach right to the heart of the music's complex and contradictory nature. This recording, of a live performance, is a superlative example of the latter. The combination of Bernstein's emotional feel for the music with the burnished sound of the Vienna Philharmonic is powerfully effective. It's an immensely dramatic reading with many telling details, like the way Bernstein creates a heavy tread in the opening funeral march by dragging the first beat of each bar. But it's much more than the sum of such details and the sense of the work as a gradually unfolding journey is brilliantly communicated.

51

Gustav Mahler

Das Lied von der Erde

Christa Ludwig (mezzo-soprano), Fritz Wunderlich (tenor);

Philharmonia Orchestra; Otto Klemperer (conductor)

EMI CDM 5 6689 2; mid-price

In the summer of 1907 Mahler's elder daughter Putzi died at the age of four, and shortly afterwards his own chronic heart condition was diagnosed. In an attempt to restore his spirits, Mahler spent a few weeks holidaying with his wife in the Tyrol. He took with him a copy of *Die Chinesische Flöte* (The Chinese Flute), a recently published German translation of ancient Chinese poetry. The poems' vivid depictions of nature and their underlying sense of the fleetingness of life made a powerful impact on him and he decided to set a selection of them to music. The result was the symphonic song-cycle *Das Lied von der Erde* (The Song of the Earth), the most deeply personal of all his works, and a summation as well as a valediction.

The six songs are divided between two soloists: a tenor and either a contralto or a baritone. The cycle begins with "Das Trinklied vom Jammer der Erde" (The Drinking Song of Earth's Sorrows), the tenor's exuberant hymn to alcoholic excess which veers between the ecstatic and the hysterical. A central orchestral section evokes the rich beauty of the world but a nagging refrain keeps returning: "Dunkel ist das Leben, ist der Tod" (Dark is life, dark is death). In "Der Einsame im Herbst" (The Lonely One in Autumn) the bleakness is subdued but more consistent. Flowing strings overlaid with the plaintive piping of an oboe create a landscape of desolation which is reinforced by the contralto's resigned and world-weary utterances.

A warmer, less complicated vision of life unfolds in the next three songs: friends chat in a pavilion; young girls gather flowers as a group of horsemen gallop by; a drunk staggers through a springtime landscape. These vignettes of Chinese life are given a decidedly Viennese flavour by the sensuous delicacy of the scoring that imbues them with an undertow of nostalgic yearning.

The final song, "Der Abschied" (The Farewell), is the longest and reaches the deepest levels of feeling. Its opening is disconcertingly stark – a low funereal knell followed by a plaintive cry from the oboe. When the contralto enters, over the stillness of a sustained low bass note, there's a feeling of terrible loneliness, despite a flute line that hovers above the voice like a bird. Mahler's use of small instrumental groupings throughout the movement has all the spareness and intensity of a Chinese scroll painting. Natural sounds are constantly conjured up – birdsong, the soft murmuring of water. His genius is to use the most exquisite sounds to suggest often quite conflicting images and emotions. But in the last pages there's a sense of reconciliation, of euphoric home-coming as the soloist celebrates earth's renewal, ending on the word "Ewig" (Eternally), which is repeated, ever more softly, like the final exhalations of a breath.

That this 1960s recording radiates such extraordinary power and clarity of feeling – despite being made over a 29-month period – is largely due to conductor Otto Klemperer's consistency of vision. Klemperer's Mahler is more sinewy and taut than most: in "Der Abschied", for instance, he brings out the oriental colouring of Mahler's instrumentation in the most vivid fashion, cajoling his instrumental soloists to produce often quite raw sounds. Similarly the strident orchestral writing of the opening song has never sounded so extreme. He's helped by having an ideal tenor in Fritz Wunderlich, who rises above the sound with heroic vigour and great beauty of tone. He's equally well served by Christa Ludwig who, though emotionally more restrained than some performers, has a true sense of the shape and direction of Mahler's long phrases and moulds them with the greatest warmth and tenderness.

52

Felix Mendelssohn

Octet for Strings; Quartet in A minor

Cleveland Quartet; Meliora Quartet

Telarc CD-80142; full price

The conductor Hans von Bülow said of Mendelssohn that he began as a genius and ended as a talent, and Mendelssohn was indeed a fantastically gifted child. A skilful painter, he also wrote fine poetry, spoke several languages, played many instruments and in 1825, aged only 16, composed one of the great chamber works – his *Octet for Strings*. With this piece he set himself the very highest of standards, and though he went on to produce much excellent music, he never again came so close to perfection.

Mendelssohn's *Octet* is scored for double string quartet, an ensemble that combined the intimacy of the quartet with the fuller sound of a small orchestra. On the score he indicated that the soft and loud markings "must be strictly observed and more strongly emphasised than is usual", and the *Octet* is a work that abounds in strong contrasts. Written in four movements, it has no weak moments. The long first-movement Allegro opens with an exuberant opening phrase that bounds along with a youthful eagerness. The movement's second subject, with its sweeter, more languid melody, introduces a subdued atmosphere that borders on the melancholic. The clouds gradually drift away in a brilliant transitional passage leading to the return of the ebullient first theme. In the Andante that follows, textures are lightened but the mood is darkened into something autumnal: it's the richest and least sentimental of all Mendelssohn's slow movements, with a depth of feeling that he reached on very few occasions.

In the wisp-like Scherzo (often used as an orchestral show-piece) Mendelssohn asks for playing that is fast but as light as possible. Inspired by lines from Goethe's *Faust* describing the motion of the clouds, the Scherzo's scampering, evanescent energy connects it with Mendelssohn's *Overture to A Midsummer Night's Dream* and the finale of his *Violin Concerto No. 2* – compositions that evoke the world of fairies and hobgoblins that was so dear to him. But it is the final movement that clinches the greatness of the *Octet* – its buoyant jubilation and tight fugal construction give it a power that's equalled by few other finales in chamber music, and the final three minutes are the most exciting thing Mendelssohn composed.

Two years later Mendelssohn wrote a remarkable string quartet in A minor whose harmonic richness and subdued melancholy reveal a debt to the late quartets of Beethoven (who had died that year). After a slow opening, the first movement is developed with a contrapuntal vigour that is typical of early Mendelssohn in the way an initial yearning quality is built to a passionate height. The slow movement possesses a quiet dignity in which the main theme is treated fugally; it is followed by a classically elegant Intermezzo, with a bustling central section, and a remarkably dramatic finale that reprises material from other movements before ending with the quartet's opening Adagio.

In this recording two of America's best string quartets join forces for a splendidly characterful performance of the *Octet*. They follow Mendelssohn's instructions to the letter, and the result is a pulsating account that goes from bold declamation to hushed intimacy in a few bars. The finale is a *tour de force*, charging along at breakneck speed but with total co-ordination between the players. The Cleveland Quartet give a no less emotional account of the A minor *String Quartet*, with a wide range of touch and timbre, and a greater emphasis on the inner voices than is usual. Especially magical is the whispered delicacy of the slow movement fugue and an almost throwaway lightness of touch in the Intermezzo.

53

Olivier Messiaen

Turangalîla Symphony

Philharmonia Orchestra; Esa-Pekka Salonen (conductor)

Sony SK66281; full price

For sixty years Olivier Messiaen – a devout Catholic – played the organ at the church of La Trinité in Paris, and much of the protean nature of his own music – its capacity to assume almost limitless shapes and colours – can be traced to the aural richness of the great Cavaillé-Coll organ there. But he was also highly receptive to much that was outside the Western musical tradition, like the metallic sounds and circular rhythms of the Javenese gamelan, and the birdsong which he transcribed and incorporated into his work.

Messiaen's richest and most colourful creation, the vast *Turangalîla Symphony*, was completed in 1948. Turangalila is a Sanskrit word combining "turanga", the speed of a galloping horse, and "lila" meaning play, in particular the play of the gods in creating the world. In Messiaen's own words "*The Turangalîla Symphony* is a love song . . . a hymn of joy . . . a joy that is superhuman, overflowing, blinding, unlimited. Love is present here in the same manner: this is a love that is fatal, irresistible, transcending everything, suppressing everything outside itself." This sense of cosmic abundance and energy is communicated by a huge orchestra of more than a hundred players that include a piano as part of a shimmering array of percussion, and an ondes martenot, an electronic instrument with a bizarre, unearthly quaver. It's a unique palette from which Messiaen creates ten dazzling, pulsating movements with a cumulative power that is overwhelming.

There's a monumental quality about much of the *Turangalîla Symphony*, partly due to the way Messiaen deploys great blocks of sound, like the heavy-footed brass theme first heard in the introductory movement, which the composer compared to the "terrifying brutality" of Mexican statuary. This sense of something ancient and ritualistic is also enhanced by Messiaen's organization of rhythm not in a way that generates a forward momentum but rather in discrete "rhythmic characters" that operate independently and sometimes in conflict with one another. It has to be said that the other-worldly dimension contributed by the ondes martenot is sometimes difficult to disassociate from Hollywood sci-fi movies of the 1950s, but Messiaen uses it in a variety of ways, most magically in the sixth movement, "Jardin du sommeil d'amour" (Garden of the Sleep of Love), where, with the strings, it forms a gentle bed of sound over which the piano wanders in imitation of birdsong. The result is an illusion of timeless floating, which for Messiaen represented the lovers Tristan and Yseult "enclosed in love's sleep". The symphony also has its moments of humour, as in the preceding movement, "Joie du sang des étoiles" (Joy of the Blood of the Stars) – "a frenetic dance of joy" according to Messiaen, but sounding like a number from a demented Broadway musical.

Pierre Boulez, Messiaen's most famous pupil, has called the *Turangalîla Symphony* "brothel music": it's an unfair jibe, but it is true that many conductors are seduced by the warm sensuousness and glittering surface of the work at the expense of all else. The great strength of Salonen's interpretation is that he realizes that these qualities are evident enough without needing to be over-emphasized. Instead he concentrates on bringing out the score's rhythmic vitality and its elementalism, at the same time revealing the heterogeneity of Messiaen's sound-world with a wondeful clarity and precision. The symphony is virtually a piano concerto, and special mention should be made of Paul Crossley's fine piano playing, which is crystalline and precise but with an appropriately fluid sense of line.

54

Claudio Monteverdi

Vespro della Beata Virgine (Vespers of the Blessed Virgin)

Sophie Marin Dagor, Maryseult Wieczorek (sopranos); Artur Stefanowicz, Fabían Schofrin (altos); Paul Agnew, Joseph Cornwell, François Piglino (tenors); Thierry Félix, Clive Bayley (basses); Les Sacqueboutiers de Toulouse; Les Arts Florissants; William Christie (conductor)

Erato 3984-23139-2; 2 CDs; full price

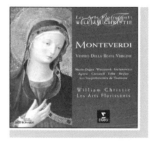

The career of Claudio Monteverdi (1567–1643) coincided with a period of profound change in European music. In their increasing concern with how best to communicate the meaning of the words they set, many composers were rejecting polyphony for a new form of music, called monody, in which the melody was confined to just one voice. Opera was one outcome of this – indeed, Monteverdi was the first great composer of opera. He also wrote many secular part-songs, called madrigals, that were initially polyphonic but became increasingly expressive in their use of dissonance and in a tendency towards a more declamatory style.

In his greatest religious work, the *Vespers* of 1610, Monteverdi had no qualms about mixing a wide variety of different styles – ancient and modern – in one piece. One reason for this eclecticism may have been because he intended the published score to be a kind of calling card and to show what he was capable of doing. After many years of working as court composer to the Gonzaga family at Mantua, Monteverdi felt over-exploited and under-appreciated. The dedication to Pope Paul V suggests that he hoped for an appointment in Rome; what he actually got – two years later – was the job of maestro di cappella (musical director) at St Mark's in Venice. Whether the *Vespers* was more than just a presentation of his skills has troubled many scholars. It is likely that music on such a lavish scale was written for a specific feast or occasion at Mantua, but nobody knows what this was.

The service of Vespers consists of an opening verse and response, followed by five antiphons, five psalms, a hymn (all of which varied according to the day), the Magnificat, and a final prayer. Monteverdi's set also includes five non-liturgical vocal pieces perhaps intended to be sung during the antiphons. These solos, duets, and trios are written in the modern monodic style and include some startlingly dramatic devices – the use of an echo in the motet "Audi coelum", the rapidly trilled ornamentation of the three tenors at the end of "Duo Seraphim". There is also some thrillingly lively instrumental playing especially in the "Sonata sopra Sancta Maria", essentially an instrumental piece over which the words "Holy Mary pray for us" are intoned in unison by the chorus.

The most immediately striking aspect of Monteverdi's *Vespers* is how theatrical and direct a work it is. The dazzling and attention-grabbing opening combines a chorus of block chords with the instrumental fanfare from his opera *L'Orfeo*. Whether performed in Mantua or Venice, Monteverdi would have used the same musicians who were performing his operas, and time and again there is an emotional immediacy in the word setting which must have been, and still is, startling in an ecclesiastical setting.

Under the direction of William Christie – a specialist in Baroque opera – the theatrical and the spiritual are perfectly reconciled. Soloists seem to have been chosen for their tonal clarity but their greatest strength is that they all sound as though they mean what they are singing. Paul Agnew, the principal tenor, gives a rapt account of "Nigra sum" without ever straining for effect. Similarly the instrumental playing has a lightness of touch and a bounce which is captivating. In the psalm settings "Laetatus sum" and "Nisi Dominus", in which the vocalists and instrumentalists perform as equals, the changes of speed are achieved with an effortless ease and everything moves along with a dance-like grace.

55

Wolfgang Amadeus Mozart

Serenade No. 10 in B flat, "Gran Partita"

Ensemble Zefiro

Auvidis Astrée E 8605; full price

In addition to all his ceremonial and concert music, Mozart also produced a sizable quantity of lighter pieces for special occasions of varying degrees of formality – often held out of doors. Such a piece was usually called a serenade or a divertimento, the two names being virtually interchangeable. This was essentially background music, against which you could eat, talk or party as the occasion demanded, but such restrictions did not prevent Mozart from writing works of great style and sophistication. *The Serenade No. 10*, the greatest of Mozart's serenades, is in seven movements, including a set of variations, and is written for the unlikely combination of twelve wind instruments and a double-bass.

Wind bands were highly fashionable in Vienna in the early 1780s – even the Emperor Joseph II had one – and several arrangements of Mozart's operas were made for such ensembles. The *Serenade No. 10*, also known (inaccurately) as the *Serenade for 13 Wind Instruments* or the "*Gran Partita*", is Mozart's wind band masterpiece. There is some doubt as to whether it was written for Mozart's own wedding celebrations in 1782 or, as seems more likely, for a benefit concert for his old friend the clarinettist Anton Stadler, held two years later. A pair of clarinets and a pair of basset horns (a lower pitched version of the clarinet) figure quite prominently, but the great glory of this work is the way all the wind instruments (two oboes, two bassoons and four horns complete the ensemble) move in and out of the limelight, dictating the varying moods of the different movements.

All the *Serenade's* movements, with the exception of the lively Rondo that closes the work, are long (the total length is about fifty minutes) and all are full of striking dramatic contrasts. Such grandness of scale was unusual in a light work, as was the rather solemn and ceremonial introduction which pitches the full ensemble, in simple sonorous chords, against a solo clarinet. It's followed by the first and stateliest of two minuets, both of which come with lighter-textured and sprightly trios. The minuets are separated by the Adagio, the emotional heart of the work. It begins unassumingly enough, with a slow lilting introduction (compared to an old squeeze-box in Peter Shaffer's play *Amadeus*) from which a long, high sustained note on the oboe suddenly appears. It's a moment of heart-melting magic, with the melody being passed back and forth between oboe, clarinet and basset horn. The fifth movement Romance is almost as beautiful: a serene and unruffled chorale-like melody that livens up in its middle section with much burbling activity from the two bassoons. The Theme and Variations that follows shows Mozart's inventiveness in terms of varying his instrumental colouring and contains another moving and aria-like Adagio, with the oboe once again to the fore.

The *Serenade No. 10* is one Mozart work that clearly benefits from being played on instruments of the eighteenth century. So-called period instruments tend to have more tonal "character" than modern ones, and occasional blips and wheezes only underline the fact that this type of music derives from the *ad hoc* wind bands of central European villages. In fact, the Ensemble Zefiro, who have recorded all of Mozart's wind music, play this work with consummate finesse while at the same time bringing out all the wit that lurks in many of the more lively passages. Also included on the disc is the *Divertimento No. 3* in B flat, a delightful piece of juvenilia that serves to reinforce just how profound a masterpiece the *Serenade No. 10* is.

56

Wolfgang Amadeus Mozart

Clarinet Concerto in A major; Clarinet Quintet in A major

Thea King (basset clarinet); English Chamber Orchestra; Jeffrey Tate
(conductor); Gabrieli String Quartet

Hyperion CDA 66199; full price

In Mozart's day the clarinet was a
relatively recent instrument – it
was invented around 1700 when
keys were added to the more rustic instrument called the
chalumeau. Mozart's enthusiasm
for the clarinet was intensified by
his friendship with Anton Stadler,
a member of the court orchestra
in Vienna who was admired for
his playing in the low register of
the clarinet and devised a downward extension of the instrument. It was for Stadler and this modified instrument – known
as the basset clarinet – that Mozart wrote his magnificent
Clarinet Quintet and *Clarinet Concerto*.

The *Clarinet Quintet* is a four-movement work combining a
clarinet with a string quartet. What is immediately striking is
how closely Mozart integrates the soloist within the group as a
whole – material flows seamlessly between them and the clarinet
usually functions as a different voice within the ensemble rather
than a dominant one. Stadler's capacity to imitate the human
voice was particularly noted by contemporary critics, and Mozart
exploits this in smooth, lyrical phrases, especially in the first two
movements. The opening Allegro is stately rather than fast, and
pensive – almost melancholy – in mood. This introspective tone
is even more marked in the tender second movement, which in

its long phrases closely resembles a rather mournful soprano aria from one of Mozart's operas. This is followed, as a contrast, by the customary minuet and trio (in this case two trios) and, in the last movement, an exceptionally mercurial set of variations.

The *Clarinet Concerto* followed two years later in 1791, making it one of Mozart's very last works. It's remarkably similar in mood to the *Clarinet Quintet* but the soloist is a stronger presence and uses the lower range of the instrument in a much more apparent fashion. There are times when the juxtaposition of the clarinet's velvety soprano tone against its more gravelly, baritonal voice suggests that two separate instruments are playing. Mozart clearly enjoyed these contrasts, and the work is marked by numerous leaps between registers, sometimes as big as two octaves. The orchestration is light (just flutes, bassoons and horns supplement the string section), and this marries well with the clarinet's clarity of sound. Like most of the piano concertos, the *Clarinet Concerto* has three movements: an easy-going Allegro with a breezy main theme; a hauntingly beautiful slow movement in which many listeners have discerned a valedictory tone; and a lively Rondo whose skittish theme really tests the soloist's skills.

Mozart gave the manuscripts of the quintet and the concerto to Stadler and they have long since disappeared. Nor for long did the basset clarinet much outlive the player who championed it, and the first printed editions of both works were scored for the conventional clarinet. This 1985 recording is one of only a few in which both works are played in revised editions for the basset clarinet, and there is no doubt that the instrument's extra range adds a new dimension to each work. Apart from this, the approach is perfectly conventional and both the accompanying ensembles are modern rather than "authentic" groups. Thea King gives a relatively self-effacing performance compared with many on the market. In the *Quintet* she is very much a first among equals, her incisive tone nicely set off by the more insinuating playing of the Gabrieli Quartet. In the more extrovert *Concerto* she manages all the technical demands with complete assurance but it's her expressive restraint that is so effective, memorably so in the slow movement, where her shaping of the elongated solo phrases is exquisite.

57

Wolfgang Amadeus Mozart

Piano Concertos No. 20 in D minor, and No. 21 in C major

András Schiff (piano); Camerata Academica des Mozarteums Salzburg; Sandor Végh (conductor)

Decca 430 510-2; full price

For the first half of his career Mozart was primarily a performer. In fact he was the first great exponent of the relatively new pianoforte, which by the second half of the eighteenth century had all but superseded the harpsichord. As a performer and teacher Mozart encouraged clarity and evenness of touch above keyboard wizardry, but he was also aware that when it came to writing piano concertos he had to find "a happy medium between what is too easy and too difficult" if he was to maintain the favour of the Viennese public. A further consideration was the fact that the pianos he played on were incapable of offering any dynamic challenge to the orchestra, so that most of his 27 piano concertos follow a simple system of exchange, whereby the orchestra plays a theme which is then repeated or developed by the pianist, and vice versa.

With the concertos initiated in 1785 by *No. 20*, Mozart began broadening the emotional range of the genre – this work in particular shows a marked darkening of mood. The menacing opening of the first movement, in which insistent syncopation contributes to a brooding tension, seems to anticipate the harsh and shadowy world of *Don Giovanni*, which was written a couple of years later. This mood is alleviated by the calm and sunny Romanze, a movement which has been criticized for being rather too placid. Almost certainly Mozart would have expected that the repeated main theme would have been ornamented by the soloist each time it returned. The finale is a breathtaking helter-skelter of a movement which opens with a dramatic upward-moving arpeggio known as a "Mannheim rocket". This movement also has shades of the last act of *Don Giovanni* in the way it contrasts furious energy with moments of comicality.

No. 21 was also written in 1785 and, like its predecessor, seems to inhabit the same harmonic world as Mozart's late operas, though here it's more *Così fan Tutte* than *Don Giovanni*. The march-like and jaunty opening soon gives way to piano writing that is especially expansive and song-like. Many people know the dreamy slow movement of this concerto, in which a glorious rising piano line is set over gently throbbing, orchestral triplets. It was used for the soundtrack of the soppy Swedish film *Elvira Madigan* and, indeed, now sometimes appears as the "Elvira Madigan" concerto on concert programmes, as if Mozart had thought up the title. The association does the concerto a disservice, for this is a serene rather than a sentimental work, full of exquisite melodies and limpid textures, only giving rein to the virtuosity expected by Viennese audiences in the brilliant passage work of the ebullient last movement.

András Schiff has recorded a complete set of Mozart's piano concertos for Decca which is among the most consistently exciting available. Modern Mozart performers tend to favour a crisp and lucid sound that emphasizes the filigree brilliance of Mozart's passage work. Schiff is no exception, but he also manages to bring a greater warmth to his playing than most. He uses a Bösendorfer piano with a well-projected but mellow sound which enables a wide range of subtle tonal variation, especially in the slow movements. His performances are helped by the exceptionally sensitive orchestral playing. Too often in these concertos, soloist and orchestra can seem too separate: here there is a real sense of a carefully worked-out balance which enables the piano to dovetail in and out of the orchestral texture with grace and elegance.

58

Wolfgang Amadeus Mozart

Symphonies Nos. 29, 35 ("Haffner") & 41 ("Jupiter")

Academy of St Martin-in-the-Fields; Neville Marriner (conductor)

Philips 446 225-2; mid-price

The first twenty or so of Mozart's 41 symphonies are the lightweight creations of an exceptionally gifted child, written largely in imitation of J.C. Bach (son of J.S. Bach), whom Mozart had got to know on his first trip to London. The turning point came in his late teens with the greater seriousness of his first symphonic masterpieces, *Nos. 25* and *29*. When he reached complete artistic maturity, during his years in Vienna, it was on piano concertos and operas that Mozart chose to concentrate. Nevertheless, his final seven symphonies – beginning with the *"Haffner"* (1783) and ending with the *"Jupiter"* (1788) – have an unprecedented grandeur and emotional depth only rivalled, at the time, by the best of Haydn.

Written in Salzburg in 1774 when he was a mere 18 years old, the *Symphony No. 29* is justifiably one of Mozart's most popular orchestral works. Its brilliant opening is instantly engaging: a simple animated phrase, set over a smooth steady line in the lower strings, moves gently up and down the first four notes of the scale. The elegant Andante and Minuet seem to look back to earlier, statelier times while the energetic finale oscillates between wit and urgency. Eight years later Mozart wrote his *Symphony No. 35* to celebrate the ennoblement of Sigmund Haffner, a family friend. This is another light but powerful work,

with a startlingly dramatic opening – this time an upwardly leaping octave which fixes the celebratory mood of a movement that
is further distinguished by its lively counterpoint (Mozart was
studying the music of J.S. Bach and Handel at the time). The
other movements more obviously reveal the symphony's origins
as an occasional, serenade-like work: a lyrical slow movement
and lively minuet are rounded off by a madcap finale that is very
close in mood to Mozart's comic operas – *Figaro* in particular.

It was the impresario J.P. Salomon who apparently conferred
the nickname "Jupiter" on Mozart's *Symphony No. 41*, which has
stuck to it ever since. It begins with a bold, attention-grabbing
phrase (complete with drums and trumpet), which is immediately answered by a phrase that is soft and ingratiating. For the second theme, Mozart returns to comic opera mode, actually
inserting the melody of an aria he'd written a few months earlier.
The Andante, marked "cantabile" (in a singing style) and played
on muted strings, is one of the most gloriously lyrical of all
Mozart's slow movements. It's followed by a Minuet remarkable
for the softness of its opening and the fluidity of its progress.
None of this prepares you for the complexity and sheer excitement of the finale. Fugal endings were fashionable in the 1780s,
but this is in a class of its own. There are no fewer than five distinct themes, which Mozart juggles throughout the movement
until, in the coda, he brings them together in a display of dazzlingly verve and invention.

Neville Marriner and the Academy of St Martin-in-the-Fields
play these three symphonies with the lightest of touches and yet
there's no lack of forcefulness when the music requires it.
Marriner was himself a violinist and the string sound of the
Academy is particularly distinguished – suave but incisive, and
with a clean sound that reveals the clarity of the Mozartian line.
This is apparent at the beginning of *No. 29* where poise and elegance are achieved by an ensemble that knows exactly how
much to hold back. The *"Jupiter"*, with its mercurial changes of
character, gets a no less convincing account that powerfully
builds to the tumultuous climax of the finale's last pages.

59

Wolfgang Amadeus Mozart

Requiem Mass in D minor

Barbara Bonney (soprano); Anne Sofie von Otter (contralto); Hans Peter
Blochwitz (tenor); Willard White (bass); Monteverdi Choir; John Eliot
Gardiner (conductor)

Philips 420 197-2; full price

Some time in July 1791 a mysterious figure called at Mozart's
lodgings in Vienna. He had come
to commission a Requiem Mass
on behalf of his master, who preferred to remain anonymous. (He
was later revealed as the eccentric
aristocrat Count von Walsegg.)
The fee was a sizeable one and,
with his wife Constanze pregnant
and numerous creditors pressing
for payment, Mozart was not in a position to refuse. But he also
had other commissions to attend to – the operas *Die Zauberflöte*
and *La clemenza di Tito*, as well as a clarinet concerto for his
friend Anton Stadler. In the end Mozart failed to complete the
Requiem before his death in early December. However, much of
the score had been written, or sketched out, and Constanze –
needing money more than ever – turned to two close associates
of her husband to complete it. Most of the work fell to the less
talented of the two, Mozart's pupil Franz Xaver Süssmayr.

Despite the circumstances surrounding its composition,
Mozart's *Requiem* is among the most powerful and moving works
he ever wrote. The opening section, Requiem aeternam, dramatically sets the tone, its stately tread (evoking the most solemn of
funeral processions) briefly punctuated by a serene soprano solo.
This contrast between gloomy, portentous sounds and bright,
consoling ones recurs throughout the work. The Kyrie, a darkly

restless fugue, functions as a kind of introduction to the longest section of the *Requiem*, the Dies irae (Day of wrath). Divided into six distinct parts, the Dies irae begins with an appropriate degree of fury from the chorus, before a trombone solo (signifying the Last Trump) heralds a sequence of solos from all four soloists, beginning with the bass and working upwards. The most thrilling music in this section, perhaps in the whole work, is the chorus "Confutatis", in which the tenors and basses rasp out a desperate description of the damned over a repeated figure in the strings, and are answered by the high notes of divided sopranos intoning the words "Voca me cum benedictis" (Call me with the blessed). It's an ethereal moment of the most astonishing beauty.

Unfortunately Mozart's draft score stops after only eight, tender bars of the Dies irae's final section, the "Lacrimosa", at which point Süssmayr takes over. After more genuine Mozart in the radiant Offertory, an inevitable sense of anti-climax sets in with the Sanctus, Benedictus and Agnus, Süssmayr's major contribution to the work. When compared to what has gone before, these sections sound at best adequate – indeed, some editions and recordings leave them out altogether. Really good performances of the *Requiem* can make the contrast in quality less obvious. Fortunately a satisfactory sense of ending is achieved in the Communion, where the music is re-cycled from the opening Requiem and Kyrie.

John Eliot Gardiner's invigorating performance sticks with the Süssmayr version, merely deleting some of the clumsier instrumental scoring. Gardiner is one of a small handful of conductors who can breathe new life into a familiar masterpiece. He is a particularly gifted choral conductor who creates a marvellously transparent and energized sound, especially suitable for the leanest and most intricate of all Mozart's major choral works. He's also gathered together four wonderful soloists: Barbara Bonney and Anne Sofie von Otter are bright-toned singers with a sensuous edge to their voices, while Hans Peter Blochwitz and Willard White exude just the right combination of authority and dignity. All four blend well together, nowhere more exquisitely than in a heartfelt account of the supplicatory "Recordare" from the Dies irae.

Arvo Pärt

Tabula Rasa; Fratres; Cantus

Gidon Kremer / Tatjana Grindenko (violin); Keith Jarrett (piano); Alfred
Schnittke (prepared piano); Berlin Philharmonic cello section; Lithuanian
Chamber Orchestra; Staatsorchester Stuttgart; Dennis Russell Davies /
Saulus Sondeckis (conductors)

ECM New Series 817 764-2; full price

Arvo Pärt was brought up in
Estonia when that country was
part of the Soviet Union and all
artists were subject to the diktats
of the Communist Party. In defiance Pärt embraced serialism (see
p.144) in the early '60s, but by the
end of the decade he started to
move in a new direction. Inspired
by his discovery of Gregorian
chant and early polyphony, Pärt
created a music that was increasingly still and meditative, a music
that – because of its simple additive techniques and religious
inspiration – has been dubbed "sacred minimalism".

In describing his own work Pärt frequently employs the term
tintinnabulation – the sound made by bells. "I have discovered that
it is enough when a single note is beautifully played. This one note,
or a silent beat, or a moment of silence, comforts me. I work with
very few elements – with one voice, with two voices. I build with
the most primitive materials – with the triad, with one specific
tonality. The three notes of a triad are like bells. And that is why I
call it tintinnabulation." Much of the timeless quality of his instrumental music derives from the fact that his harmony does not
modulate (change key) and so there is none of that sense of movement towards a climax that exists in nearly all post-Renaissance

music. That is not to say that this music is entirely static, merely that its energy seems permanently rooted in the present.

Today Pärt is most celebrated for his choral works, but it was with three orchestral pieces that he made his initial impact in the West. The first of these was the short but powerful *Cantus in Memory of Benjamin Britten* (1976). Scored for string orchestra and tubular bells, the *Cantus* is paradoxically both austere and enormously rich. It is built around a slow descending minor scale – reminiscent of Britten's ballad "Old Abram Brown is Dead and Gone" – that is interspersed with the slow tolling of bells. As the music gradually slows down, it intensifies in volume before the strings cease, leaving the thin but resonant echo of a lone bell.

Fratres, written the following year, is an equally sombre work in which a chorale-like melody is repeated over a drone. The occasional beat of a drum underlines the processional quality of the work and its title surely hints at a monastic inspiration. It was originally written for the Estonian early music ensemble Hortus Musicus but Pärt has subsequently made a number of versions for different instrumental combinations. *Tabula Rasa*, also written in the late 1970s, is another work based on a hypnotic series of repetitions. An animated flurry of strings – like a group of people moving towards you – is punctuated by static and subdued moments for violin and prepared piano. The second half is more contemplative: slow-moving and ethereal strings answered by the bell-like middle register of the piano.

This recording caused an enormous stir of interest when it was released in 1984. Many who heard it were transfixed by the simplicity and the emphasis on a pure and beautiful sound, and the recording became known as much through word of mouth as through any critical response. Two versions of *Fratres* are performed here: an exceptionally sombre one by twelve cellists of the Berlin Philharmonic and a more animated and restless version by violinist Gidon Kremer and pianist Keith Jarrett. The most intense piece, however, is the short *Cantus*, whose rich overlapping lines resonate in the memory long after the music has stopped.

61

Giovanni Battista Pergolesi

Stabat Mater

Véronique Gens (soprano); Gérard Lesne (alto); Il Seminario musicale

Virgin Veritas VC5 45291-2; full price

The *Stabat Mater* is an anonymous thirteenth-century poetic meditation detailing the suffering of the Virgin Mary as she witnesses her dying son on the cross. The deeply mournful and compassionate character of the work has appealed to many composers: Palestrina set it, as did Vivaldi, Rossini, Dvořák and, more recently, Arvo Pärt. But of all the numerous versions of the *Stabat Mater*, few are more beautiful or so emotionally charged as the one by Giovanni Battista Pergolesi (1710–1736).

Pergolesi's short life was spent mainly in Naples, a major centre for opera, where a style had developed that emphasized the beauty and virtuosity of the solo voice. Pergolesi tried hard to establish himself as a composer of *opera seria* (a genre devoted chiefly to historical or mythological themes) but in the end he proved much more popular as a writer of comic operas, one of which – *La serva padrona* – achieved great fame and is still performed today. He also wrote a number of religious works for various Naples churches, which include two settings of the mass, two of the antiphon *Salve Regina*, as well as the *Stabat Mater*.

Written in 1735, shortly before the fatal onset of tuberculosis forced his retirement to a Franciscan monastery at neighbouring Pozzuoli, the *Stabat Mater* is without doubt Pergolesi's masterpiece. It's an extremely sensitive response to the text, in which the dramatic use of pauses and of clashing notes (dissonance) is much in evidence. If it sounds rather operatic for a religious work, this is largely because Pergolesi dispenses altogether with a chorus in order to present the text through the more immediate solo voice: each of the twelve sections is allocated either to the soprano or the alto or to both in duet. The music is extremely varied given that the prevailing mood is one of pain and supplication. Pergolesi has no qualms about changing styles from one movement to the next: the subdued, meditative opening duet, for example, is very obviously a piece of church music but it is immediately followed by an aria which seems a flamboyantly dramatic expression of anguish. There are even some moments of relative lightness, with the verse beginning "Quae morebat et dolebat" (Who mourned and grieved) set as a sprightly, almost comic, alto solo. But it was Pergolesi's emotional expressiveness rather than his versatility that so impressed his contemporaries – J.S. Bach made an arrangement of the *Stabat Mater* while Jean-Jacques Rousseau described its opening as "the most perfect and most touching to have come from the pen of any musician".

Many recordings of Pergolesi's *Stabat Mater* tend to sentimentalize it by using a lush orchestral sound and big, operatic female voices. More recently, in the name of greater authenticity, there has been a tendency to pare down the accompaniment and use a male alto with a female soprano (the original performance would almost certainly have employed a castrato for the upper part). With Véronique Gens and Gérard Lesne – who also directs – you get a near-perfect balance of well-rounded voices that emphasizes the sensual quality of the music. There's an intimate balance between the two singers and the instruments which is enhanced by the use of a theorbo (a large lute) instead of a harpsichord continuo. In addition, Lesne gives a beautifully judged performance of the second *Salve Regina* and there's a sparkling account of a short cello concerto, the last movement of which was later used by Stravinsky in his witty homage to Baroque music, the ballet *Pulcinella* (see p.177).

62

Pérotin

The Hilliard Ensemble; Paul Hillier (director)

ECM 837 751-2; full price

Up to the time of Pérotin (c.1170–c.1236), the predominant music of the Christian church had been monophonic chanting – the singing of a single line of music by one voice or by several voices. In its simplest form this became known as plainsong, and several different versions of it existed, the best known of which is Gregorian Chant. Some time in the ninth century another voice, with its own independent line of music, was added, a development that marks the beginnings of polyphony (a term that literally means many sounds). At first it was very simple: the added line moved at a fixed interval in parallel to the plainsong melody, usually beneath it. This simple polyphony was called *organum*; the plainsong melody was called the *cantus firmus* (fixed song); the voice that sang it was the *vox principalis* and the added voice the *vox organalis*.

Parallel duplication of the melody was obviously limited in its appeal, and more ambitious variants soon began to appear. One especially important development was that the added voice (the *duplum*), instead of moving note on-note with the plainsong melody, was placed on top of it and made rhythmically independent and melodically more complex, employing as many as twenty notes to one in the lower part. This style was called florid or melismatic organum and it existed alongside the older note-on-note style.

The earliest composers of polyphonic music whose names have come down to us are Léonin (c.1159–1201) and Pérotin, both of whom were part of an extraordinary flowering of culture and scholarship that took place in Paris in the late twelfth century. Léonin's music was written down in the *Magnus liber organi* (Great Book of Organum), which Pérotin later edited and added to. Very little is known of their lives but they almost certainly had some connection with the new cathedral of Notre Dame. Léonin's music is relatively simple two-part writing, whereas Pérotin embraced the more ambitious florid style, writing in three, and sometimes four, parts – strange but utterly compulsive music, in which harmonic plainness is pushed along by a free-flowing rhythmic suppleness, each phrase coming to a halt in an austerely simple cadence.

In Pérotin's hands florid organum became increasingly lively and exciting: two of his most striking contributions to the genre, the extraordinary *Viderunt omnes* and *Sederunt principes*, are the earliest examples of Western music written for four independent voices. Both pieces contain startlingly dance-like rhythms in the higher voices, which lilt and weave their way around the drawn-out line of the plainsong *cantus firmus*, echoing each other's material in a way that dissolves the dominant melodic line to create, in Paul Hillier's words, "a kaleidoscope of constantly shifting textures".

Paul Hillier, the director of the consistently excellent Hilliard Ensemble (an all-male group), never treats this music as an archaeological curiosity. On the contrary, the performances are direct and deeply moving, the impeccably well-balanced and wonderfully flexible singing creating an image of the Gothic as something delicate and light-filled – an approach complemented by ECM's marvellously spacious sound. There are nine pieces on this disc (six are by Pérotin and three are anonymous) of varying degrees of complexity and for various combinations of voices. What they all have in common is a radiant clarity and a sense of joy that belies the idea that early Christian music is necessarily something static and solemn. The one minor irritation of this outstanding disc is that the sleeve-notes include the Latin texts but do not provide translations of them. But ultimately the precise meaning of the words is less important than the fluid and rapturous sounds.

63

Sergei Prokofiev

Piano Sonata No. 7

Maurizio Pollini (piano)

Deutsche Grammophon 419 202-2; with music by Stravinsky, Webern & Boulez; mid-price

Prokofiev was a brilliant pianist and his earliest compositions were written in order to show off his prodigious talent. At his St Petersburg début, in 1908, he was hailed by progressives and damned by conservatives, and thereafter rapidly established a reputation as the *enfant terrible* of the avant-garde. What caused such a sensation was the way Prokofiev had no qualms about using the piano in an aggressively percussive and rhythmically dynamic fashion, a defining characteristic of his piano writing throughout his career as a composer.

His finest works for solo piano, *Sonatas Nos. 6, 7* and *8*, were all begun in the late summer of 1939. Of the three, the *Sonata No. 7* is the most celebrated, having become one of the few uncompromisingly modern solo works to have entered the core repertoire for pianists. It was completed in 1942, as the Germans were invading Russia, and was first performed by Sviatoslav Richter in January 1943. It begins with an Allegro inquieto which, according to Richter, "immediately throws one into the anxious situation of a world losing its equilibrium. Anxiety and uncertainty reign." This is achieved by a rapidly scuttling figuration in the right hand, brittle in tone, which sometimes takes on the quality of a demented march. Brief respite is provided by calmer, slower music that appears twice, but the mood is still edgy and unstable and the movement ends as nervously as it began.

The slow movement has provoked much comment. For many the brooding lyricism of its main theme, so clearly indebted to the early nineteenth century (Chopin and Schumann both spring to mind), seems incongruously sweet in the context of the sonata's outer movements. In fact the music has a profoundly tragic undertow to it, and the harmonies often create an austere and angular effect particularly in the more anguished central section. The final movement (marked "Precipitato") is a furious *moto perpetuo*, one moment suggesting some elemental force, the next something brutal and machine-like. Its driving 7/8 rhythm may have been suggested by Georgian folk dance, but even so it's hard to understand how music this raw was acceptable to the Soviet cultural commissars. The probable explanation is that artistic expression of pain and anguish was regarded as legitimate during the extreme privations of World War II. In any case, the *Sonata No. 7* was a great popular success and Prokofiev was rewarded with a prestigious Stalin Prize.

Maurizio Pollini is a markedly unsentimental pianist, famed for his brilliant technique, the clarity of his playing and his abiding sense of the overall shape and direction of a work. It's an intellectual but never a dry approach to music-making, which yields spectacular results in this 1971 recording of the *Sonata No. 7* – the most exciting currently available. There are no false touches in this account: the outer movements possess just the right amount of dramatic energy without being clamorous and he is one of the few pianists who has no difficulty in integrating the central movement into the general scheme of things.

The rest of this astounding disc is given over to other major twentieth-century piano works, including a scintillating account of Stravinsky's piano transcription of three sections from his ballet *Petrushka*. With Webern's *Variations for Piano* and Pierre Boulez's *Second Piano Sonata* you enter much more abstract terrain. Webern's music is pared down to the point of austerity, and combines a severe sense of order with sudden gestures of a more expressive freedom. The Boulez sonata is for the most part a profoundly destructive assault on the keyboard – uncomfortable listening even in Pollini's fastidiously accurate rendition.

64

Sergei Prokofiev

Alexander Nevsky; Lieutenant Kijé

Elena Obraztsova (mezzo-soprano); London Symphony Orchestra & Chorus; Chicago Symphony Orchestra; Claudio Abbado (conductor)

Deutsche Grammophon 447 419-2; mid price

Prokofiev, like Stravinsky, received his musical training in St Petersburg before the Revolution, but unlike Stravinsky he decided to return to Russia in 1933, after many years of living in Paris. In the West Prokofiev was regarded as a Modernist and an innovator; in the Soviet Union such terms were used by officials to denigrate artists who were perceived as not toeing the party line.

One of Prokofiev's first jobs on his return to the Soviet Union was to write the music for Alexander Feinzimmer's satirical film *Lieutenant Kijé*. Set in the reign of Tsar Paul I, it tells the story of a non-existent army officer (created as the result of an ink blot on an official document) who succeeds in rising through the ranks. It was Prokofiev's first film but his sensitivity to the medium was immediate and the film's initial parade-ground montage is an audio-visual *tour de force*. Unfortunately it was withdrawn for political reasons, so Prokofiev turned the music into an orchestral suite. It's a light and witty work in five movements, and shows off his brilliant gifts as a melodist. The tone is set by the graphic orchestration: a distant cornet, followed by fifes and drums, represents Kijé's birth. This is followed by a set of variations on a mock-melancholy Russian song, a jolly cornet solo over an oompah bass for Kijé's wedding, and the famous troika ride music complete with jingling bells. Kijé's death is a wonderful mélange of overlapping themes in which most of the previous material is reprised.

Prokofiev's next film score was for *Alexander Nevsky*, made in 1938 by Sergei Eisenstein. Both men regarded music as an integral element of a film and worked closely together, even editing some of the footage to music that had already been recorded. Set in the thirteenth century, the film tells of the invading Teutonic Knights, their subsequent atrocities and their defeat on the frozen Lake Chud by the Grand Duke Alexander. The following year Prokofiev condensed the 21 sections of music into a seven-part cantata for mezzo-soprano, chorus and orchestra. In both film and cantata the climax of the work is the "Battle on the Ice", a hugely exciting sequence in which a bleak landscape is evoked prior to the mounting approach of the knights and the chaotic sounds of battle. This is genuinely terrifying music, with Prokofiev brilliantly communicating a sense of terrible menace and ensuing violence. It is followed by an intense and beautiful lament by a young woman (mezzo-soprano) wandering the corpse-strewn battlefield in search of her lover. These two sections form the heart of a work which concludes with a victory hymn sung in triumph over pealing bells and an array of jangling percussion.

In the wrong hands *Alexander Nevsky* can sound like crude and hectoring propaganda (it received a boost as a patriotic work when the Nazis invaded Russia) but Abbado and his forces give a superbly musical (as well as dynamic) performance with a forceful LSO chorus managing to sound convincingly Russian and Elena Obraztsova highly touching in her aria. In *Lieutenant Kijé* Abbado is partnered by the Chicago Symphony Orchestra, who turn in a superbly crisp and effervescent account. As an added bonus the same orchestra perform the *Scythian Suite* of 1916, which began life as a Russian Ballet commission. This is Prokofiev in primitive mode (Stravinsky's *Rite of Spring* firmly in mind) and its propulsive energy is delivered with a ferocious impact from an orchestra in top form.

65

Henry Purcell

Ode for St Cecilia's Day: Hail, Bright Cecilia!

Gabrieli Consort and Players; Paul McCreesh (conductor)

Archiv 445 882-2; full price

St Cecilia, a martyr of the second century, did not acquire her widespread status as the patron saint of music till the Renaissance, and it was not until 1683 that her saint's day, November 22, became the occasion for annual celebration. The group of London musicians who instigated the first St Cecilia's Day commemoration included Henry Purcell, the greatest composer England has ever produced. The celebrations consisted of a church service, followed by a banquet at which an ode, specially written and set to music, was performed. In 1692 Purcell's second contribution, *Hail, Bright Cecilia!*, outstripped all previous offerings in scale and splendour.

Purcell came from a family of professional musicians. His father and his uncle were both musicians at the court of Charles II, where, as a result of the king's exile in France, a more cosmopolitan flavour had been introduced into English music. Part of Purcell's achievement was his success in synthesizing certain formal aspects of the French style with the more lyrical and expressive style of the Italians. What makes his music unique, however, is the way these elements are suffused by a sense of national identity, typified by heavy chromaticism, elaborate counterpoint, extended melody and, above all, emotional immediacy.

He rapidly became England's most revered composer, famed, in the words of a contemporary, for "having a peculiar Genius to express the Energy of English Words". Nicholas Brady's verses for

Hail, Bright Cecilia! are mediocre, but with Purcell it was often the case that the more lacklustre the words the more imaginative was his response. Here it certainly was: so much so that the first audience demanded to hear the whole thing all over again.

The ode is scored for the grandest of forces – an orchestra of strings, recorders, oboes, trumpets and kettledrums, six soloists and a six-part choir – and begins with a long orchestral sinfonia, after which a varied succession of solos, ensemble and choruses begins to unfold. The profoundest music is reserved for the text's more speculative moments, in particular the extraordinary solo "'Tis Nature's voice" which describes the emotional impact music has on the listener. It was written for a high male voice as an incredibly free-flowing and heavily ornamented declamation and may have been performed by Purcell himself at the first performance. It's followed by a rousing chorus, "Soul of the World", in which the divided choir – their division suggesting the "scatter'd atoms" of the text – overlap a broad, noble melody which turns into a fugue before all the voices come together on the words "perfect harmony". The ensuing musical vignettes of individual instruments ("the airy violin", "the Am'rous flute", etc) are largely conjured up in order to show their inferiority to that "Wondrous machine" the organ (the instrument at which St Cecilia is usually depicted), which is described in an extremely jaunty bass solo. A final chorus brings all the forces together in a triumphant homage to the "Great Patroness of Us and Harmony!"

A completely satisfactory performance of this work is extremely hard to bring off. This 1994 recording comes closer than most. Its outstanding quality is the sheer energy and élan of the orchestra and chorus, who never let you forget that this is a festive work. They are greatly aided by Paul McCreesh's choice of speeds, which tend toward the brisk without ever sounding rushed – the opening sinfonia is particularly invigorating. The soloists, who are enlisted from the chorus, are good and occasionally outstanding. Best of all is the bass Peter Harvey, who projects just the right degree of expressiveness in what is a highly theatrical work.

66

Jean-Philippe Rameau

"Les Indes Galantes" Suite

Orchestra of the Eighteenth Century; Frans Bruggen (conductor)

Philips 438 946-2; full price

Jean-Philippe Rameau is an indisputably great composer whose achievements are only fully appreciated in his native France. This is largely because nearly all his most important music was written for the highly artificial world of Baroque opera, and in modern times Handel is the only Baroque composer whose work has translated well onto the modern stage. But to miss out on Rameau's music is to deprive oneself of a unique voice. More so than either of his two great contemporaries, Bach and Handel, Rameau was an outstanding orchestrator who could create the most vivid, and sometimes bizarre, impressions by his deft handling of instrumental colour alone. In many of the instrumental sections of his operas there's a brilliant pictorial imagination on display.

Born in Dijon, Rameau spent his early career as a cathedral organist and gained more of a reputation as a theorist than as a composer. In 1723 he arrived in Paris but achieved little before being taken up by the financier La Riche de la Pouplinière, one of the wealthiest men in France. La Pouplinière's contacts and money launched Rameau on his late-flourishing operatic career. His first opera, the classical tragedy *Hippolyte et Aricie*, made a huge impact but created a storm of controversy because it dared to challenge the stiff formal conventions of French opera with something more emotionally real and musically exciting.

It was followed, in 1735, by *Les Indes galantes*, a peculiarly French form of theatrical spectacle called an an opéra-ballet, in which dance was as important as song. Made up, in its final form, of a prologue and four acts, the opera takes place in Turkey, Peru, Persia and America and tells four separate stories of the triumph of love over adversity. The fashionable exoticism of *Les Indes galantes* allowed Rameau to display his mastery of a wide range of dance forms. Between the conventional formality of the opening overture and the ceremonial splendour of the chaconne with which it ends, there's a medley of highly contrasted pieces including pastiches of what would now be called world music. Thus you hear the droning of French bagpipes in the "Musette en rondeau" and the pounding of a Provençal drum in the equally rustic "Contredanse". Better known is "L'air pour les Sauvages", whose hard-driven jauntiness is said to have been inspired by the singing and dancing of two Louisiana Indians.

Les Indes galantes also contains some highly atmospheric moments, like the furious downward rush of the violins representing the North Wind, or – most magically of all – the brilliant evocation of dawn in "L'air pour l'adoration du soleil". The ethereality of this last piece is achieved by a combination of strings with flutes and piccolos, and a striking feature of *Les Indes galantes* is the importance of the woodwind instruments which don't just add colour to a piece but are often used to carry the melodic line as well.

It is not unusual to extract the dances from *Les Indes galantes* to form a separate orchestral suite, although losing the narrative context tends to create the impression of a kaleidoscope of disparate musical sound-bites darting restlessly from one mood to the next. Frans Bruggen's selection and his measured direction of the work restores a sense of order to the proceedings. He doesn't underline the agitated or the odd, as do some Rameau specialists, but lets the music unfold graciously and naturally. What comes across is how the brilliance of Rameau's orchestral colouring creates the most alluring combination of elegance and passion.

67

Maurice Ravel

Piano Concerto in G

Arturo Benedetti Michelangeli (piano); Philharmonia Orchestra; Ettore Gracis (conductor)

EMI CDC7 49326 2; full price

Ravel the Impressionist, the composer of such sensuous masterpieces as the song-cycle *Shéhérazade* and the *String Quartet*, had an obverse side – urbane, witty and at times rather brittle – that came increasingly to the fore as the years passed. What united these aspects of his personality was Ravel's genius as an orchestrator, his ability to sustain a musical argument through strikingly varied and unpredictable instrumental colour. Nowhere can this be seen to more brilliant effect than in his last major work, the *Piano Concerto in G*, written and first performed in 1932.

A literal crack of the whip sets the first movement in motion and the initial impression is similar to the start of Stravinsky's *Petrushka* – a feeling of excitement and the bustle of a milling crowd. The skittish opening melody is stated first by the piccolo (the piano simply adding to the orchestral texture) and then by the trumpet. Things have slowed down by the time the piano enters as soloist proper with an initially languid theme that seems to combine a Spanish flavour with a hint of the blues. In fact a jazz element colours much of the two outer movements, and there is more than a hint of Gershwin about the piano writing's jerky syncopations, "blue" notes and rapid passage work. However, Ravel's orchestration is entirely his own, full of startling touches like the sudden ghostly harp solo that occurs two-thirds of the way through the first movement, followed by equally mysterious piano trills that seem to glide from note to note.

If the first movement is, in the main, a joyful hubbub of clamorous voices, then the slow movement is one of chaste austerity. It begins with the piano alone: the right hand delivering a plaintive, almost apologetic, melody over a simple left-hand accompaniment. Ravel claims to have been inspired by the slow movement of Mozart's *Clarinet Quintet*, but the effect is more like a stripped-down Chopin nocturne. The orchestral entry maintains the subdued mood before the piano takes on the role of accompanist, notably providing a delicate filigree of high notes over the oboe's re-statement of the main theme. The madcap finale begins with a drum-roll and a mini fanfare, as if announcing the entry of clowns into a circus ring. There's certainly a degree of manic comicality here, with a hard-driven piano part, overlaid by some shrill woodwind writing, which rushes to an increasingly hysterical conclusion.

Few pianists have brought such finesse and purity of line to this concerto as Arturo Benedetti Michelangeli, yet he never loses sight of Ravel's dictum that "The music of a concerto . . . should be lighthearted and brilliant, and not aim at profundity or at dramatic effects." This, at least, is true of the way he treats the outer movements, finding just the right balance between poise and elasticity while dovetailing into the orchestral texture whenever appropriate – and with more modesty than many pianists. The slow movement is a different matter: here Michelangeli finds real sadness in Ravel's simple song, exposing the Romantic heart beneath the cool exterior.

Michelangeli couples the Ravel concerto with the last and least famous of Rachmaninov's four piano concertos. It occupies a completely different world from the Ravel, a world full of heart-tugging emotional rhetoric in which the piano leads and the orchestra merely fills in the gaps. But despite its rather incoherent nature, there's a more muted and tragic quality to this concerto than the more celebrated second and third, and it's this that Michelangeli taps into, producing an account that is the most convincing on record.

68

Steve Reich

Music for 18 Musicians

Steve Reich and musicians

ECM New Series 821 417-2; full price

Minimalism is the name given to the music of a group of American composers who from the 1960s reacted against the orthodoxies of the European avant-garde and the chance processes of John Cage to create music in which insistent phrasal repetition is the most obvious defining characteristic. The term was first applied to them by the English critic and composer Michael Nyman, adopting it from the visual arts where it had been applied to the stripped-down work of American artists like the sculptor Donald Judd and the painter Frank Stella. Nyman saw a parallel in the music of LaMonte Young, Terry Riley, Steve Reich and Philip Glass. In their early work these composers employed the most minimal means a limited number of pitches, a fairly constant density of texture, and regularity of pulse. The effect was of a pattern of sound in which changes occured but in a way that was often difficult for the listener to discern precisely.

Repetition has always existed in Western music, perhaps most obviously in the work of Baroque composers, but also in the music of early polyphonists like Pérotin (see p.123), whose religious music had little sense of destination. Reich has declared his admiration for both Bach and Pérotin but he was also attracted to non-Western musics, especially the pitched percussion of Indonesian gamelan orchestras and West African drumming. This welter of influences finds its most coherent and brilliant expression in *Music for 18 Musicians* (1974–76), a work that took Minimalism into the mainstream. Reich's early works had been rather austere, more concerned with process than with sound, but in *Music for 18 Musicians* his main concern "was making beautiful music above everything else" and his instrumentation is much more adventurous, combining percussion instruments – pianos, marimbas, xylophones and metallophone – with strings, clarinets and wordless vocals. The result is a continuum of vibrant, shimmering layers of sound which suggest the movement of sunlight on water and the pulsating life beneath the surface. Throughout the work there's a distinct contrast between the rhythm of the percussion and the rhythm of the other instruments, which is dictated by the duration of a breath, "one breath after another gradually washing up like waves against the constant rhythm of the pianos and mallet instruments."

Music for 18 Musicians provides a deeply paradoxical listening experience: on the one hand there is something trance-like in the unresolved and directionless nature of the chords (Reich divides the work into eleven sections, each based around a different chord), but on the other hand the limited harmonies make one acutely aware of changes in rhythm and dynamics – in particular the way different instruments move in and out of the foreground. It possesses a throbbing, invigorating energy while achieving moments of mantra-like peacefulness. It should be said that some find the repetition extremely irritating, and if you listen to it expecting something to happen in a conventional way you may well be frustrated. This is music that demands a kind of unconscious awareness, a listening that is more like a form of contemplation. On this recording, Reich and his musicians perform – from memory – with a breathtaking energy and precision. Despite the regular chugging pulse, the sound is never mechanistic and there's a real sense of joy and purpose in the playing. Details of instrumental timbre are well served by ECM's engineers, with the warm throatiness of the bass clarinets showing up particularly well. Reich was also involved in mixing the recording, and the sound is consistently clear and bright.

69

Nikolai Rimsky-Korsakov

Scheherazade

Beecham Choral Society; Royal Philharmonic Orchestra; Thomas
Beecham (conductor)

EMI CDM5 66983 2; with Borodin's *Polovtsian Dances*; mid-price

Rimsky-Korsakov is renowned for
many achievements: he was an
inspirational teacher (of Stravinsky,
for one); he was an expert orchestrator of other composers' music
(including a lot of Mussorgsky);
and he did much to emancipate
Russian music from Western influence, forging an aesthetic based on
native melodies and harmonies. As
a composer, however, his interna-
tional fame rests on a single work, the symphonic fantasy
Scheherazade.

Many of Rimsky-Korsakov's operas and orchestral works are
based on Russian folk material, but he had a typically nineteenth-century predilection for what was perceived as the exoticism of Islamic cultures. Composed in 1888, twenty years after
his Eastern-flavoured symphonic poem *Antar*, *Scheherazade* is
Rimsky-Korsakov's response to *The Thousand and One Nights*,
whose eponymous heroine saves her own life through her virtuosity as a story-teller. Convinced of the falseness of women,
Sultan Shariyar has decided to execute each of his wives after
their wedding night. Scheherazade saves herself by entertaining
him with such mesmerizing stories that after one thousand and
one nights of postponing her death (in order to hear how the
stories will end) he finally relents altogether. In his autobiography Rimsky-Korsakov wrote of *Scheherazade*: "All I desired was
that the hearer, if he liked my piece as symphonic music, should

carry away the impression that it is beyond doubt an Oriental narrative of some numerous and varied fairy-tale wonders, and not merely four pieces played one after another and composed on the basis of themes common to all four movements."

With its lush and dramatic music, its cinematic scene changes and mood swings, *Scheherazade* does indeed suggest a convoluted narrative, an impression reinforced by the titles ascribed to each of the movements: "The Sea and the Vessel of Sinbad", "The Tale of the Prince Kalender", "The Young Prince and the Young Princess" and "Festival at Bagdad". But Rimsky-Korsakov was always ambiguous about how literally he wanted the music to be heard, and he later withdrew the titles. The most obvious way the four episodes are tied together are the two motifs which the composer identified as the voices of the Sultan – big and brassy – and Scheherazade – a beguiling and sinuous violin solo that weaves its way through the work. Essentially each movement centres on one or two big tunes which are developed through vivid and varied orchestration and a lot of repetition. The last movement – in which many of the previous themes re-appear – is the most exciting, its initial hustle and bustle eclipsed by a tumultuous climax at the heart of the movement before the languid "voice" of the violin, and the "once upon a time" chords that opened the work, bring it to a close.

The fame of *Scheherazade* came about largely as a result of it being mounted as a ballet by Diaghilev's Russian Ballet in 1910. The combined impact of the music, Bakst's opulent designs and Nijinsky's animal magnetism caused a sensation. Thomas Beecham, whose father funded the company in London, loved this music. He conducted it for Diaghilev in 1912 (adopting tempi that were considered too rapid by the dancers) and recorded it nearly half a century later, in 1958. This disc stands out for the energy of his conducting and the virtuoso playing of the RPO including the beautifully judged solo violin of Steven Staryck. Beecham's sheer delight in the spectacle of the music marks this out as one of his finest studio recordings. In addition, the accompanying *Polovtsian Dances* from Borodin's opera *Prince Igor* are given a performance of unbridled power.

70

Camille Saint-Saëns

Symphony No. 3; Carnaval des Animaux

Peter Hurford (organ); Montréal Symphony Orchestra / London Sinfonietta;
Pascal Rogé & Cristina Ortiz (pianos); Charles Dutoit (conductor)

Decca 430 720-2; full price

Saint-Saëns is one of those composers to whom things came a little too easily. An infant prodigy on a par with Mozart and Mendelssohn, he could churn out melodies with astonishing facility, with the result that much of his work is routine and predictable. Though pilloried by the likes of Debussy and Ravel, Saint-Saëns is – in his finest music – a hugely entertaining composer, who frequently quickens the pulse even if he rarely touches the heart.

The barnstorming *Symphony No. 3* shows him at his crowd-pleasing best, despite some fairly obvious shortcomings. French composers tended to be self-conscious about writing symphonies, regarding them as an essentially German genre that was unsuitable to their lyric gifts, and certainly Saint-Saëns' third is a work in which spontaneity is more important than structure: there's no shortage of sparkling melodic material but the themes tend to be piled up, one after the other, with little or no sense of development. The symphony's opening is powerfully atmospheric: two darkly lugubrious string chords are followed by brief woodwind solos before pizzicati in the low strings lead into a theme of nervous restlessness that recalls Schubert's *"Unfinished" Symphony* and the Dies irae motif that Berlioz employs in his *Symphonie Fantastique*. This theme recurs throughout the work in various disguises, functioning as a not entirely convincing unifying element. The warmly sentimental Adagio that follows has an almost Mahlerian gravitas, partly through the solemn underpinning provided by the organ part.

The third movement is a spine-tingling Scherzo, urgent and compelling, that seems to have strayed in from a lost work by Berlioz. Its lighter central section rather startlingly introduces a pair of pianos who bring an air of carnival jollity to the proceedings. The main theme returns, then transforms itself into a grandiose fugue that gradually thins out almost to nothing before a massive C major chord on the organ heralds the start of the final movement. This is an utterly thrilling hodge-podge of ideas – a fugal introduction, glittering passage work, triumphant fanfares, the return of the Dies irae theme – which concludes with a very long and very loud organ chord.

The *Symphony No. 3* was first performed in London in 1886, the same year that Saint-Saëns wrote his *Carnaval des Animaux* as an amusement for his friends. (Performances were forbidden during his lifetime in case it detracted from his reputation.) Scored for two pianos and small orchestra, its fourteen sections depict a wide range of creatures including *Persons with Long Ears* and *Pianists*, the latter represented by irritatingly repeated scales. Saint-Saëns' humour is often deft and satirical – *Tortoises* get to amble along to a version of Offenbach's can-can played extremely slowly, *Elephants* receive similar treatment, to a dance by Berlioz. There are also moments of great magic: the singing cello melody of *The Swan* (made famous by the ballerina Pavlova) and, most beautiful of all, the rippling arpeggios of the mysterious *Aquarium*.

Recorded in the resonant acoustic of Montréal's St Eustache church, this muscular account of *Symphony No. 3* packs a real punch. Organ and orchestra have been well balanced and Peter Hurford's choice of registration means that he moves in and out of the limelight with an unobtrusive ease save for the shattering opening to the finale. Dutoit brings out all the freshness of Saint-Saëns' orchestral colouring with the vital timpani part having just the requisite bite. He is never indulgent and the Adagio is especially moving because of his restraint. In the *Carnaval* Cristina Ortiz and Pascal Rogé knock sparks off each other in a witty, sensuous and utterly scintillating performance.

71

Domenico Scarlatti /
George Frideric Handel

Sonatas and Suites

Murray Perahia (piano)

Sony SK62785; full price

George Frideric Handel and Domenico Scarlatti were both fantastically gifted keyboard players, and their skills were put to the test against each other when Handel visited Italy as a young man. The two first met in Venice in 1701, then in Rome a year later, where the musical contest was staged. Honours were divided: Scarlatti seems to have been adjudged the better harpsichordist, Handel the more talented organist. Thereafter their careers diverged dramatically. Handel headed for England, where he wrote on the grand scale – operas, oratorios and orchestral music. Scarlatti finished up teaching music to the Infanta Maria Barbara of Portugal before accompanying her to Madrid when she became Queen of Spain in 1729.

It was for Maria Barbara that Scarlatti composed the bulk of his 555 keyboard sonatas, each of which is made up of a single movement in two repeatable sections. They are an astonishing achievement: brilliantly inventive, often very demanding technically, and with a wonderful diversity of moods, ranging from the fiery to the melancholic. Many of them are marked by the colour and character of popular Spanish music: dance rhythms abound, harmonies sometimes recall gypsy song, and in many passages the repetition of a single note or of the same phrase suggests the strumming of a guitar or even the clacking of castanets.

Handel's keyboard music is much more conventional. Most of it is written in the form of suites – a sequence of some five or six movements usually based on dance forms. In 1720 he published an edition of eight such suites that are widely regarded as the cream of his solo keyboard compositions and which include the well-known set of variations nicknamed *"The Harmonious Blacksmith"*, which closes *Suite No. 5*. This is supremely elegant music with an unruffled courtliness even in the fast movements. There is none of Scarlatti's quicksilver flights of fancy – instead each line of music has a boldness and a clarity, and there is a prevailing sense of each movement developing out of the music that preceded it.

Nothing divides classical music connoisseurs more than the issue of whether such music is more appropriately played on a modern piano or on a harpsichord. The main differences between the two instruments are that the strings of the harpsichord are plucked while the piano's are struck by a felted hammer, and that the harpsichord's tone and dynamics cannot be varied by the pressure of the performer's fingers, unlike the piano's. Thus the harpsichord sound is essentially bright but somewhat mechanical – "two skeletons copulating on a tin roof" is how Sir Thomas Beecham memorably described it – whereas the piano is more mellow and, arguably, more expressive. Murray Perahia's 1996 recording of three Handel suites and seven Scarlatti sonatas makes a powerful case for the piano. Unlike some pianists who play Baroque music, there is never any suggestion of him trying to mimic the sound of the harpsichord. Playing on a very mellow-toned instrument, his miraculously varied touch and judicious pedalling produce a kaleidoscopic range of tonal colouring and shading. This is especially appropriate in the Scarlatti sonatas, where the different strands of the music demand what one Scarlatti expert has called "imaginary orchestration". Perahia's subtle dynamics also bring an added dimension to the music, particularly in the B minor sonata, where an insistently repeated phrase, which figures in both halves of the sonata, is made even more mysterious by an exquisitely judged diminuendo. This is exceptionally refined and beautiful playing in which virtuosity is always at the service of the music rather than a means of self-advertisement.

72

Arnold Schoenberg

Verklärte Nacht; Variations for Orchestra

Berlin Philharmonic; Herbert von Karajan (conductor)

Deutsche Grammophon 415 326-2; full price

Schoenberg was a crucial figure in the crisis of tonality that occurred at the end of the nineteenth century. Music's traditional basis in the major and minor scales had been challenged by Wagner in his opera *Tristan and Isolde*, in which he allowed the harmony to drift in every direction, only returning to the key note of the scale at the end of each act. This tonal destabilization – by using notes outside of the scale – was called chromaticism, and it became a defining element of late Romantic music. On examining Schoenberg's first major work, *Verklärte Nacht* (Transfigured Night), one academic described it as looking "as if someone had smeared the score of *Tristan* while the ink was still wet."

Written in 1899 for string sextet, *Verklärte Nacht* is based on a poem by Richard Dehmel. In a moonlit wood, a woman tells her lover that she's pregnant by another man. He replies that their love for each other will transfigure the unborn child and make it their own. Schoenberg's musical response is a brilliant sequence of thematic metamorphoses, coloured by a heavy sensuousness that epitomizes a distinctively *fin de siècle* obsession with sex and spirituality. An incredibly dark and weary atmosphere is conjured up by the opening low descending scale. The mood of suffocation and anxiety becomes more pronounced throughout the first half, but in the second a more rhapsodic tone develops, culminating in the ecstatic music of the transfigured night. The lushness of the sound became even more pronounced when Schoenberg arranged the work for string orchestra in 1943.

For all its chromaticism, *Verklärte Nacht* is still a melodic work. Ten years later Schoenberg made the leap into atonality – that is, into music which has no tonal centre. This freedom produced his most extreme works but by the early 1920s he wanted to return to a more systematic form of composition and so devised what became known as twelve-tone music or serialism. In a serialist work the twelve notes of the chromatic scale are fixed by the composer in a particular order called a tone row. This row may be manipulated (inverted, reversed, etc) but it remains a constant element and generates all the melodies and harmonies of the work.

Schoenberg's intellectualism has earned him a reputation as a dry composer but the first impression of the *Variations for Orchestra*, his first serialist orchestral work, is the delicacy of much of its sound-world – his orchestration includes a xylophone, mandolin and a flexatone (a percussion instrument with a sound like a musical saw). You cannot hear the variations taking place – Schoenberg himself said that this was impossible – but you can detect an underlying momentum generated by the music's complex rhythmic patterns, and the rich orchestral detail builds to a climax as fulfilling as that of any conventional variation sequence. The more often you hear this piece, the more easy it becomes to follow the many layers of which it is constructed and so appreciate its fundamentally classical architecture.

The riotous 1928 premiere of the *Variations for Orchestra* was performed by the Berlin Philharmonic. Nearly fifty years later, when this record was made, the orchestra clearly had this music in its system. This is an immaculately detailed performance in which Schoenberg's layering of sounds is revealed with translucent clarity. In the more opulent world of *Verklärte Nacht*, the performance is no less meticulous. Instead of luxuriating in the velvety richness of the 1943 version, Karajan goes for subtlety, carefully pacing the orchestra so that by the time the coda is reached, the feeling of transcendence is all the more uplifting.

73

Franz Schubert

Sonata No. 21; Twelve German Dances; Allegretto in C minor

Stephen Kovacevich (piano)

EMI CDC5 55359-2; full price

Almost alone among the great composers for the piano, Schubert was himself no virtuoso. This is reflected in the relative absence of bravura passages in his piano works – with the exception of the *Wanderer Fantasy*, none of them makes technical demands that put them beyond the reach of any but the preternaturally gifted. Instead his method was more ruminative and gentle, concerned above all with nuances of feeling. Schubert translated his matchless lyric gift into practically everything he wrote for the piano, from the numerous lighthearted dance pieces (twelve of which are included on this disc) to the profoundly personal late sonatas. It is with the sonatas that his reputation as a piano composer stands, even though they were completely neglected for a hundred years after his death until certain pianists, notably Artur Schnabel, resurrected them.

The greatest of Schubert's piano works is the last of a group of three sonatas he completed just a month or so before he died. In the intensity of their expression, these three are often compared to the late piano sonatas of Beethoven. But whereas Beethoven's late sonatas are marked by a desperate need to communicate, Schubert's look inward, constantly repeating and reformulating themes as if they were persistent memories. In these long musical soliloquies, the forceful direction of Beethoven's music is replaced by structures that seem to circle round their subjects without ever coming to rest. This is especially true of the first movement of the B flat sonata (*No. 21*), in which the opening melody radiates a feeling of unruffled serenity before ending in a long, low trill that suggests something dark and foreboding. It's a profoundly meditative movement – one moment dreamy, the next bold and defiant – that can suggest the depths of anguish or exude a calm acceptance depending on who is playing it.

More than the overtly Romantic piano repertoire of Schumann or Liszt, Schubert's piano sonatas – especially the B flat – permit the performer a lot of scope in the definition of details of mood. Some pianists tend to play up the Romantic agony, underlining the desperation with slow speeds and dramatic pauses, others are more understated, emphasizing the lyricism rather than the frailty of Schubert's melodies. Stephen Kovacevich certainly falls more into the former than the latter category, but there is no trace of self-indulgence in his performance. The actual piano sound is warm and embracing, and Kovacevich uses the pedals to create some wonderfully subtle transitions from light to shade in the long first movement. But there's enormous variety in his touch and the movement's more playful second subject is handled with exquisite delicacy.

The second movement Andante is one of the saddest episodes Schubert ever wrote. A gentle rocking accompaniment intensifies the somnambulistic mood of the main melody which opens and closes the movement. There's a brief moment of reassurance in the song-like second section but essentially this is a movement of quiet despair. It's followed by a Scherzo of magical lightness which is almost shocking compared with what's gone before, though under Kovacevich's fingers there are hints of darkness even here, especially in the dance-like middle section with its odd lurching accents. The final Allegro is more obviously ambiguous: a harsh unharmonized note announces its opening and frequently interrupts the movement's forward momentum. There's a constant tension between major and minor, the lyrical and the clamorous, that Kovacevich always makes sound entirely cogent rather than capricious, and which culminates in a brilliant but manic coda with, perhaps, a rather hollow ring at its centre.

74

Franz Schubert

Winterreise

Dietrich Fischer-Dieskau (baritone); Jorge Demus (piano)

Deutsche Grammophon 447 421-2; mid-price

Vienna in the early nineteenth century was music mad. As well as all the public concerts, weekly *soirées musicales* were held in upper-middle-class homes at which chamber music, piano solos and, of course, songs (Lieder, in German) could be heard. During his short life Schubert composed more than six hundred such songs, transforming what was essentially trivial salon fare into a vehicle for the most profound and complex feelings.

In 1823, during a time of great distress caused by the onset of syphilis, Schubert discovered a collection of verses, *Poems from the Posthumous Papers of a Travelling Hornplayer*, by the little-known Wilhelm Müller. The poems' folk-like directness made a strong impact on him and he set twenty of them as a cycle entitled *Die schöne Müllerin* (The Fair Maid of the Mill). The simple story – a young miller setting out on his travels – became in Schubert's hands a universal tale of disenchanted innocence.

Four years later he returned to the same collection for a second song cycle, *Winterreise* (Winter Journey), in which the despondency that closed *Die schöne Müllerin* is pushed to extremes. His friends heard the complete cycle in the autumn of 1827 and were dismayed by its bleakness. Schubert had altered the order of Müller's 24 verses, so that the rare flashes of consolation provided by the poet were no longer apparent. There is no real narrative: we simply follow the protagonist, a world-weary and rejected lover, in his lonely wanderings through the snow-bound countryside.

Unlike the earlier cycle, *Winterreise* depicts nature as something cruel and unsympathetic to the traveller's fate. As his journey progresses, so his vision becomes more inward and his surroundings take on an oppressive symbolism. The cumulative power of the work is achieved through the most subtle, and often simple, musical details – the recurrent steady beat conveying the traveller's plodding footsteps, for instance, or the sudden change from minor to major in the last stanza of the first song, intensifying the mood of quiet desperation. And then there's the way the accompaniment is often used for the sharpest of scene-painting, like the restless passage work conveying the wind in *Die Wetterfahne* (The Weather-vane) or the underlying triplets that so brilliantly suggest the wheeling presence of the crow in the song of that name. The final song, *Der Leiermann*, is a master-stroke: the traveller meets a destitute hurdy-gurdy player (the first human contact in the cycle), whose rustic music Schubert mimics with a drone and a quirky figure in the piano. The wanderer wonders whether to go with him but his question is left hanging in the air and the song simply drifts away.

More than anything he wrote, Schubert's songs live or die with the talents of their performers. Like the plays of Shakespeare (several of whose verses he set) they respond to a variety of interpretations while always needing someone who can strike the right balance between characterization and vocal beauty. Few singers have identified so strongly with Schubert's songs as the baritone Dietrich Fischer-Dieskau. Communicating the textual meaning of a song, with every detail and nuance revealed, is of paramount importance to him and his Lieder interpretations are always unforgettably vital and committed – indeed, too much so for some critics. Fischer-Dieskau has recorded *Winterreise* no fewer than eight times. This performance dates from 1966 when the singer was in his early forties, and the combination of a rich and authoritative vocal sound with mature interpretative insights is completely convincing. Jorge Demus, his sensitive accompanist, is more reticent than most, but this simply highlights the emotional veracity of Fischer-Dieskau's performance.

75

Franz Schubert

String Quintet; Symphony No. 5

Isaac Stern and Alexander Schneider (violins), Milton Katims (viola), Pablo Casals and Paul Tortelier (cellos); Prades Festival Orchestra; Pablo Casals (conductor)

Sony SMK 58992; mid-price

Schubert's *String Quintet* in C major, his greatest chamber work, was also his last – it was on October 2, 1828, just seven weeks before his death, that the composer wrote to a friend that he had "finally turned out" a quintet. Schubert revered the string quintets of Mozart, but rather than adopt the same format of string quartet plus extra viola, he scored his work for an extra cello, thus creating a darker, more sonorous tone for this beautiful and tragic work. This is music that is not simply sad – it's a tangible embodiment of a struggle for spiritual peace, particularly in the profound Adagio, a movement as powerfully communicative as anything Schubert ever wrote.

The *Quintet* is a big work in every sense. Its opening Allegro possesses a breadth and an expansiveness which is due partly to the weight given by the added bass instrument, but also to the richness of the melodic invention. The two come together in the glorious second subject, with the cellos lyrically serenading in close intervals over an insistent background rhythm. Schubert's handling of the instrumental balance is masterly: one minute he creates a texture of almost orchestral dimensions, the next he switches to a more transparent and vulnerable sound. Vulnerability is the first impression created by the Adagio, with Schubert spreading out the instruments and alloting them different types of sound: a piping short-breathed phrase for the violin, sustained chords in the middle voices, and pizzicato from the second cello. This movement is the emotional core of the work, a desperately poignant, valedictory statement whose fractured and turbulent central section only heightens the feeling of inner calm when the main theme returns.

The last two movements, the Scherzo and final Allegretto, both have something of the whirl of the dance floor to them. Scherzos are usually pretty boisterous movements, but this one is more tempestuous than most, although the Trio that goes with it is an exceptionally sombre and introspective affair with a really thick and heavy sound to it. The finale is the most carefree movement, an infectiously lively dance that relaxes into a more ingratiating lyricism in its second subject. There's a distinctly Viennese feel to this movement, as if Schubert wished to pay tribute to his native city's inexhaustible appetite for airy music, but it in no way undermines the deep seriousness that has gone before.

This 1952 recording shows that great chamber music performances are not the exclusive domain of musicians who have played together for many years. It was recorded during the Prades Festival in southern France, where the legendary Spanish cellist Pablo Casals was living in voluntary exile as a protest against the fascist dictatorship then governing Spain. The artists involved were all highly talented and very individual musicians and, despite the boxy mono sound, this recording truly deserves its status as a classic. There's a palpable rapport between the performers that comes across with amazing force – the slow movement, in particular, has an extraordinary quality of timelessness about it. It's also a very emotional performance, with first violinist Stern and Casals employing techniques, such as sliding between the notes, which today would be regarded as suspect. Even the extraordinary groaning noises that periodically emanate from the 76-year-old Casals only reinforce the unique sense of occasion. The fill-up is a hitherto unreleased recording of Casals conducting Schubert's youthful *Symphony No. 5* at Prades in 1953. It's an adequate performance, but it lacks the musical alchemy so evident in the performance of the *Quintet*.

76

Franz Schubert

Symphonies No. 3 and No. 8 ("Unfinished")

Vienna Philharmonic Orchestra; Carlos Kleiber (conductor)

Deutsche Grammophon 449 747-2; mid-price

As a composer trying to make his name in his native Vienna, Franz Schubert lived in the shadow of Beethoven, and yet his nine symphonies owe less to Beethoven's style than might be expected. Devoid of the Promethean defiance that's so prevalent in Beethoven's works, they are generally lighter and more expansive, and have a thematic profusion that owes more to Haydn and Mozart than to Beethoven. While it's true that Schubert's symphonies, as a whole, are not as individualistic as his smaller-scale works, their range of emotion – from capricious gaiety to the deepest melancholy – marks them out as one of the greatest of all symphonic cycles

On this exhilarating disc, conductor Carlos Kleiber has chosen to make an unusual but extremely effective coupling of the youthful and relatively unknown *Symphony No. 3* with the overwhelmingly tragic *Symphony No. 8*, better known as the *"Unfinished"*. It would be hard to find two more different pieces of music. The third symphony, written when Schubert was just seventeen, is a sunny and effervescent work despite its rather portentous introductory Adagio. Influences are easy to identify: Haydn in the dainty Allegretto (which Kleiber takes far faster than most); early Beethoven in the forceful Minuet; while the madcap finale suggests a particularly farcical scene from a comic opera.

Eight years later came the eighth symphony, one of Schubert's supreme orchestral masterpieces, which with its brooding power became a model for the Romantic composers of the next generation. Why he abandoned this work, having only completed the first two movements, is a mystery, though various theories have been suggested, including the idea that he found himself unable to continue after discovering that he had syphilis. The fact that it's unfinished has not affected its popularity, despite its being one of Schubert's most profoundly gloomy creations. An air of fatality is immediately apparent in the arresting opening, in which cellos and basses play a darkly hued theme of ominous power. This leads into a nervy rustle of strings over which a yearning melody is played by oboe and clarinet in unison; then the movement's main idea is introduced, in the shape of an almost jaunty theme stated initially by the cellos. This theme dominates the proceedings but repeated statements of the movement's chilly opening means that an air of bleakness is never far away.

The second movement is a more open-air episode, in which the previous movement's intimations of doom are initially transformed into a mood of optimism. However, two minutes into the movement and this serenity gives way to something more hesitant – a plaintive extended phrase on the clarinet with a "sobbing" motif in the accompaniment is suddenly exploded by a fortissimo scurry of strings and percussion. It's a shattering and uncharacteristically angry moment that dramatically reinforces the mood of uneasiness that runs throughout the whole symphony.

This sense of duality – confidence versus anxiety, calmness versus agitation – is something that Carlos Kleiber brilliantly points up in this recording. He's partnered by one of the world's most refined orchestras, the Vienna Philharmonic, and yet it is not so much the sound quality that hits you (good though that is) as the crackle of excitement and tension that Kleiber elicits from the orchestra. The *"Unfinished"* is a very familiar work and many recordings give the impression of conductor and orchestra going through the motions – with Kleiber, however, the emotional temperature is raised to such an extent that it is like hearing the work for the first time.

77

Robert Schumann

Fantasie in C; Fantasiestücke

Martha Argerich (piano)

EMI CDM 7 63576 2; full price

"Everything extraordinary that happens impresses me and impels me to express it in music," Robert Schumann once wrote, and much of his music serves as an autobiography for his troubled psyche. As a young man the defining moment of Schumann's life came when he fell in love with Clara, the brilliant daughter of his piano teacher Friedrich Wieck. The emotional upheaval caused by the couple's burgeoning love and Wieck's unrelenting opposition to it were sublimated by Schumann into a series of outstanding piano works composed between 1835 and 1840 – the year they eventually married. Though Schumann had unbounded respect for his forebears, these works are quintessentially Romantic in their extra-musical inspiration, their episodic construction and in the volatility of their emotions.

The genre of the fantasia (or fantasie) had existed since the Renaissance as a free-form piece that was extemporized rather than composed. For the Romantics it signified a work in which the imagination was completely liberated. The *Fantasiestücke* (Fantasy Pieces) of 1837 is typical of Schumann's penchant for assembling a miscellany of poetic miniatures into an extended work. It's a collection of eight interconnected pieces that conjure up flickering visions of twilight, confused dreams, a lover's hopes and anxieties. Schumann added titles after the music was written: thus a gentle lullaby becomes *Des Abends* (At Evening), a fleet-footed whirl of Chopinesque virtuosity *Traumes Wirren* (Dream Confusion). Most evocative of all, and Schumann's favourite, is *In der Nacht* (In the Night), in which delicate undulating lines suggested to him the play of the waves around Leander as he swam to his lover across the Hellespont.

The fact that the *Fantasie* was meant as both a coded love letter to Clara and a homage to Beethoven is a key to its compelling mixture of intimacy and grandeur. Intended as a fund-raising contribution for a proposed Beethoven monument, the *Fantasie* began life as a sonata in three movements entitled "Ruins, Trophies, Palms". Although the three movements were retained, the work mutated into something profoundly anti-classical in its breathless turbulence and tonal ambiguity. The first movement is the most radical: a disorientating rush of semiquavers in the left hand is met, in the right, by a theme (the "Clara" theme) which is both ardent and defiant. Schumann described it to Clara as "the most passionate thing I have ever composed – a deep lament for you." Moods and emotions constantly fluctuate – a new solemn theme marked "In the manner of a Legend" brings a short-lived tranquillity before a quotation from a Beethoven love song signals the movement's final air of resignation. The remaining movements have more stability: the second begins as an exuberant march – proud and confident – that is propelled forward by an obsessive bouncing rhythm in its second half; the slow finale, on the other hand, recalls Beethoven in its sombre, sonorous opening which gradually builds to a climax of unalloyed rapture.

Martha Argerich, one of the supreme interpreters of Romantic piano music, seems to have a special rapport with the music of Schumann. The music's impulsive poetry seems to correspond perfectly to her spontaneity and passionate energy. In the *Fantasie*'s titanic first movement the sudden shifts and changes of directions are so perfectly judged that it's as if she is thinking the music into being. The *Fantasiestücke* is no less magical, and, once again, it's her intuitive responsiveness to each piece's internal dynamic that brings them so vividly to life – a sudden change of emphasis that brings out an inner voice, or a broadening of pace that moderates the music's restless momentum.

78

Robert Schumann / Edvard Grieg

Piano Concertos

Stephen Kovacevich (piano); BBC Symphony Orchestra; Colin Davis (conductor)

Philips 446 192-2; mid-price

In the nineteenth century, being a professional pianist and being a composer for the piano were virtually synonymous activities. The exception to this rule was Schumann, whose potentially brilliant career as a pianist was over by 1832, due to an injury to his right hand. Whether this was caused by the early stages of syphilis or by the overuse of a mechanical device meant to strengthen the fingers, is still a matter of argument. Fortunately, Schumann was able to turn to his wife Clara as a ready and willing interpreter of his piano music. Doubly fortunate, in that Clara was one of the greatest pianists of the mid-century.

Both Clara's playing and Robert's music eschewed virtuosity for its own sake. Beginning work on a *Phantasie* for piano and orchestra in 1841, Schumann described it to Clara as "something between a symphony, a concerto and a grand sonata . . . I cannot write a virtuoso concerto and must think up something different." What was different about it was the way that the piano and orchestra were closely integrated, their exchanges often having the intimacy of a chamber work. The work begins with a brief declamatory flourish from the piano, before the orchestra states the plaintive main theme with the oboe carrying the melody. The intially serene mood is replaced by one of greater urgency, propelled by flowing accompanying figurations in the piano part and culminating in a dramatic, but pointedly unflashy, cadenza.

The *Phantasie* was rejected by publishers and so became the first movement of the *Piano Concerto*, with the other two movements added in 1845. In place of the conventional introspective slow movement, Schumann provides a short Intermezzo that opens with the sprightliest of three-note motifs before a more passionate theme is introduced by the cellos. A brief echo of the concerto's initial theme acts as a link into the finale, the most free-ranging and kaleidoscopic of the three movements. As in the first movement there's a constant sense of the piano pushing the proceedings along that culminates in the most exuberant of codas.

The Norwegian composer Edvard Grieg wrote one of the most popular of all piano concertos in 1868 while holidaying with his wife in Denmark. Closely modelled on that of Schumann, it is is in the same key (A minor), and begins with a similar attention-grabbing flourish from the piano that leads into an orchestral statement of the wistful first theme. The major difference is that Grieg seems much more eager to please – there's a richer array of melodies which lie closer to the surface of the music, and it is not without its moments of Lisztian flamboyance. The Adagio boasts a touchingly beautiful melody – sombre in its orchestral form, gloriously refulgent in its piano version. The work closes with a spirited rondo containing at its centre an extremely tender new theme that is triumphantly re-stated at the work's conclusion.

These two concertos are frequently coupled together on the same disc, even though their differences are as distinctive as their similarities. Stephen Kovacevich is more alert to this fact than many pianists, and the Grieg gets a markedly more extrovert treatment than the Schumann. In the latter, Kovacevich is especially subtle in the way he moves in and out of the orchestral texture, knowing exactly when to hold back and when to assert himself. He's well supported by Colin Davis, one of the most sensitive of concerto conductors, and the obvious rapport between pianist and conductor makes for a wonderful fluidity in the outer movements.

79

Dimitri Shostakovich

String Quartets Nos. 3, 7 and 8

Borodin String Quartet

Virgin VC7 59041-2; full price

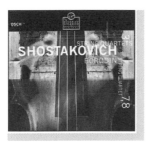

If the symphony was the arena in which Shostakovich made his public utterances (albeit often ambiguously), then the string quartet was the place where he expressed his more private thoughts and emotions. He wrote a total of fifteen, beginning in 1938 with a quartet that is extremely simple, as if he were tentatively feeling his way into a new genre. An intimate, confessional mode is characteristic of many of them, but as a cycle they possess a great deal of variety and (as with the symphonies) much of their impact comes from Shostakovich's practice of placing seemingly incongruous elements in disconcerting juxtaposition.

The *Quartet No. 3* of 1946 is an oddly fragmented and elusive work despite the clarity of its texture. It starts in sprightly enough fashion but the studied jollity of its opening folk dance is never convincing, while the two ensuing movements are openly peevish, featuring mechanistic repetition in the Moderato and aggressive dance rhythms over grunting cellos in the Scherzo. Even the bleakly elegiac slow movement has a distracted, absent feel to it. With the finale this sense of disorientation is at its most pronounced, in the way the argument wanders from one unrelated episode to the next, failing to find root in any of them.

Shostakovich's wife Nina died in 1954, and the *Quartet No. 7* was written six years later as a memorial to her. It's an extremely spare and concentrated work, full of strikingly vivid touches. There's a witty interplay between bowed and plucked strings in a first movement that is propelled along by a distinctly nervous energy. The Lento is a haunted lament, the first violin singing its grief over the second violin's gently undulating line. Panic and anxiety pervade the furious rush of the finale before it subsides into wan recollection of the first movement theme and three restful closing chords.

Even more "autobiographical" is the *Quartet No. 8*, written during a visit to the bomb-damaged city of Dresden, supposedly in response to what Shostakovich saw there. It's now thought to be more of an account of the composer's own personal nightmare, and it's littered with quotations and self-references, including repeated statements of Shostakovich's own musical signature, the notes D, S (E flat), C and H (B natural). It's an immensely sombre work, with three of its five movements marked Largo (slow). The DSCH motif begins and ends the quartet, in darkly brooding fugal passages reminiscent of the late quartets of Beethoven. The second and third movements are both fast, the former exuding all the frantic desperation of a hunted animal, the latter a ghostly waltz-time *danse macabre*. The penultimate movement, another Largo, is the saddest of all. It begins with three hammer-like blows over a long sustained note but is, in the main, a prolonged sigh of yearning which quotes poignantly from a revolutionary song "Exhausted by the hardships of prison".

Shostakovich was fortunate to have two of the best Soviet quartets on hand to play his string quartets – the Beethoven Quartet, who premiered them, and the Borodin Quartet, who gave their second performances. It's the Borodin recordings that really established the reputation of the quartets in the West, and the group have recorded them all several times. This disc, however, is not part of a complete cycle, but a one-off made for Virgin in 1991. It's an extremely bold and dynamic performance, which never flinches from the often harsh sounds that Shostakovich calls for, and gets right to the heart of the quartet's edgy, introverted world.

80

Dimitri Shostakovich

Symphony No. 5

Scottish National Orchestra; Neeme Järvi (conductor)

Chandos CHAN 8650; full price

To what extent Shostakovich maintained his artistic integrity during the years of Stalin's tyranny is a matter of debate. At his funeral in 1975 he was accorded full honours as a People's Artist of the USSR, but since then many of his colleagues have testified that much of his music possessed complex layers of meaning: that while on one level it conformed to the banal criteria of his political masters, on another it criticized and mocked the Soviet system through cryptic musical messages.

Of all the works whose meaning has been pored over since his death, the *Symphony No. 5* has aroused most controversy. Written in 1937, a year after *Pravda* had condemned his opera *Lady Macbeth of Mtsensk* as "musical chaos", the symphony was Shostakovich's chance to redeem himself by writing a work that fitted the "objective" and optimistic ideals of Socialist Realism. At the premiere in Leningrad, the audience's reaction was unequivocal: people wept through the slow movement and the work received a standing ovation. At the suggestion of a journalist, Shostakovich agreed that the symphony should be sub-titled "A Soviet Artist's Reply to Just Criticism", and the authorities seemed satisfied.

Yet, even if you don't know the background, the *Symphony No. 5* is far from being a straightforward work. Like Mahler (whom he greatly admired), Shostakovich often tended to juxtapose startlingly different types of music in a way that could destabilize the prevailing mood. Thus in the symphony's spare opening, high and low strings create a feeling of bleakness and fragility. A strumming accompaniment reinforces the sense of directionlessness before a sudden menacing entry of piano and horns pushes the music into a realm of high tension. The screw is increasingly tightened, climaxing with the arrival of a crudely strident march (a portrait of Stalin?), before the subdued, twilight world of the opening quietly reasserts itself.

The short Scherzo that follows is uncannily close to Mahler, but at the same time is shot through with touches of grotesquerie that are typical of Shostakovich's black humour. The funereal Largo forms the emotional core of the work; its long-breathed phrases, which gradually build in volume, suggest a mood of loss and ennervation. Brass instruments are conspicuously absent, and a sense of quietly mounting desperation gradually emerges in the second half. The quietness is shattered by the finale, another manic march that sounds gloriously triumphant to some ears, hysterical to others. But even during the most "positive" moments there's a nervous edge to the music, as in the serene horn melody that is undermined by wavering high violins. Soviet critics saw the symphony's clamorous ending, with its insistent repetition of high As, as an exultant hymn to conformity. Shostakovich apparently felt otherwise, and in his posthumous memoirs (whose authenticity some have questioned) he is quoted as saying "It's as if someone were beating you with a stick and saying, 'Your business is rejoicing, your business is rejoicing' . . . What kind of apotheosis is that?"

The Estonian Neeme Järvi studied with Yevgeny Mravinsky, who conducted the very first performance of the *Symphony No. 5*. He is not as austere and hard-driven a conductor as his teacher, but there's a similar tautness in this 1988 performance with the Scottish National Orchestra. Especially impressive is the restraint with which Järvi handles the slow movement's desolate ebb and flow, and the way he builds the last movement to its final profoundly ambiguous conclusion. The disc also includes the *Suite No. 5* from the 1931 factory ballet *The Bolt*, an example of Shostakovich's inventive wit, even when faced with the most propagandist of scenarios.

81

Jean Sibelius / Carl Nielsen

Violin Concertos

Cho-Liang Lin (violin); Philharmonia Orchestra / Swedish Radio Symphony
Orchestra; Esa-Pekka Salonen (conductor)

Sony SK44548; full price

It's not altogether surprising that
Jean Sibelius and Carl Nielsen are
often bracketed together: they are
both Scandinavian, were born in
the same year, and have reputa-
tions based on ambitious and
highly regarded symphonic cycles.
They were also both excellent
violinists – Sibelius was good
enough to audition for the Vienna
Philharmonic, while Nielsen
played for several years in the Royal Theatre Orchestra in
Copenhagen – and both put their knowledge of the instrument
to good use in writing a violin concerto. These two works, however, pinpoint the profound differences in their music.

Sibelius's concerto got off to a terrible start, receiving such a
mauling after its premiere in 1903 that the composer made
extensive revisions, partly to balance the roles of the soloist and
the orchestra, but also to make the solo part more playable. (The
original soloist's manifest problems with the score undoubtedly
had a bearing on its poor reception.) It is now one of the most
popular concertos in the repertoire, albeit one that violinists still
approach with caution.

A boldly Romantic work, the Sibelius concerto has a glorious
opening, with the soloist's drawn-out, Slavic melody emerging
plaintively over tremolo strings. The solo part is very demanding
and includes some immensely difficult, but thrillingly rhapsodic,

double-stopping (whereby two strings are played at the same time). The slow movement is essentially a song. After a mysterious introduction in which the woodwind play in thirds, the ardently lyrical melody begins low on the instrument and rises higher and higher – always on the instrument's lower two strings – against a melancholy background of horn and bassoon. Like the first movement, however, there is an urgent, ominous undertow to the movement that emerges in its second half. In the finale Sibelius finally allows sunlight to penetrate the shadows in the work's dynamic finale. The critic Donald Tovey referred to this movement as "a polonaise for polar bears", a joke that gives an idea of the orchestral music's enjoyably lumbering gait but scarcely does justice to the soloist's scintillatingly brilliant contribution in which the very highest level of virtuosity is demanded.

Nielsen was fortunate in that his *Violin Concerto*, completed in 1911, was championed by an outstanding violinist, his son-in-law Emil Telmányi. A buoyant and expansive work, it deserves to be better known than it is. Constructed in two sections, it pitches soloist (and listener) straight into the action with an extended cadenza which leads into the first movement proper, an episode of great variety, mainly optimistic but with moments of an almost Elgarian wistfulness. This mood is developed in the second section where a ruminative and subdued theme is exchanged, at first between soloist and woodwind and then with the whole orchestra. The work ends with a rather quirky Rondo which is Bartók-like in its repressed energy and hints at the kind of village band music that Nielsen himself used to play.

Cho-Liang Lin gives brilliant accounts of both concertos. The Sibelius is an immensely subtle reading with an exemplary balance between soloist and orchestra – the first movement, in particular, conveys a powerful sense of the violin as an optimistic, but still troubled, voice emerging from the dark orchestral texture. In the Nielsen, Lin's articulation and phrasing are immaculate but what is especially impressive is the way he avoids a vibrato-thick tone in favour of an emphasis on a clear line. In both works he's helped by extremely sympathetic orchestral playing and by a natural-sounding balance that never over-favours the soloist.

82

Jean Sibelius

Symphonies Nos. 5 and 7

City of Birmingham Symphony Orchestra; Simon Rattle (conductor)

EMI CDM7 6422 2; full price

Sibelius's ardent nationalism is an obvious presence in tone poems such as *Tapiola* or *The Swan of Tuonela*, both of which took their inspiration from the *Kalevala*, the Finnish national epic. Attempting to trace national characteristics in Sibelius's seven symphonies – his greatest achievement – is more difficult: they have no hidden narratives and there are no traces of folk song or even of folk-style themes within them. What they do possess is an epic sweep and a cleanness in the rich orchestral sound that one tends instinctively to associate with the austere and elemental landscape of his native land.

The most popular of the symphonies is the *Symphony No. 5*, a work of which the composer himself thought very highly. The first draft was completed during World War I, at a time when financial pressure was compelling Sibelius to turn out a considerable volume of music. Sibelius found this heavy workload unbearable ("I cannot become a prolific writer. It would mean killing my art") and withdrew into seclusion, devoting nearly all his time to the revision of his new symphony. In a letter to his friend Axel Carpelan he wrote: "In a deep mire again. But I begin already to see the mountain that I shall certainly ascend . . . God opens his door for a moment and His orchestra plays the *Fifth Symphony*." In the end Sibelius revised the piece twice, completing the final three-movement version in 1919.

The defining quality of the symphony is its concision, and it is a near-perfect example of Sibelius's technique of creating delicate and complex structures from simple means. In this case, each of the movements begins with a chord from which all the subsequent material is developed. There is a Wagnerian weight to this work, with its dominant brass and a last movement that boasts a glorious leading theme, neatly characterized by one critic as "Thor swinging his hammer". The conclusion is probably the composer's most radiant and dramatic: a thunderous chord appears to signify the movement's end, but as it dies away another crashing chord is struck, and so it goes on until, after the sixth chord, the work's tonality is brought full circle in a final cadence.

The *Symphony No. 7*, completed in 1924, represents the summit of Sibelius's search for symphonic fluency. The work's four movements are played as one piece: vestiges of the traditional symphonic structure − such as a Scherzo and an Adagio − are discernible, but the development of the material is so tight and its progress so inevitable that the music seems to grow organically from the ominous rising string theme with which the work begins. If the fifth symphony is an essentially confident and optimistic work then the seventh is more ambivalent, with a overriding sense of restless struggle between opposing forces that is exemplified, about halfway through, by a swirling "whirlwind" motif in the strings, over which the steady presence of the brass intones.

Simon Rattle is one of the most exciting of modern Sibelius conductors and his reading of *Symphony No. 5* reveals a refinement and a structural integrity that are enormously impressive. He gets a rich, burnished sound from his orchestra, with some wonderful brass playing, and the climactic final movement is breathtakingly exciting. The more complicated *Symphony No. 7* is also pulled off with similar panache: the steady build-up possesses an inexorable and steely logic, with each idea spaciously unfolding out of the previous one. Rattle brings out the sinewy clarity of Sibelius's orchestration while never stinting on the work's tumultuous emotionalism.

83

Bedřich Smetana / Alexander Borodin

String Quartet No. 1 / String Quartet No. 2

Takács Quartet

Decca 452 239-2; full price

The reputation of the Czech composer Bedřich Smetana is based on his opera *The Bartered Bride* and the cycle of symphonic poems *Má Vlast* (My Homeland), two large-scale pieces that typify his preoccupation with the expression of national identity – a concern common to many Central and Eastern European composers in the nineteenth century. For his more private statements Smetana turned to chamber music, and in his *String Quartet No. 1* (subtitled "From My Life") he attempted nothing less than a musical autobiography.

It was written in 1876, two years after a syphilitic infection had resulted in total deafness. It's a bitter-sweet work, with pleasant youthful memories seen from a perspective of isolation and frustration. A declamatory falling fifth from the viola acts as an ominous "fate" motif and the initial mood of the first movement has a frantic edge to it that gradually lightens with the arrival of a more gentle and yearning second theme. Smetana's youthful love of dancing is represented in the second movement – earthy polkas in the outer sections, more refined music in the central trio. The tender slow movement is his homage to his wife: a mournful cello solo leads into a wistful melody that builds to an increasingly impassioned lyricism. The finale illustrates, in Smetana's words, "how to make use of the element of national music, joy at the outcome of following this path". This joy is interrupted, however, by the catastrophe of deafness – a shattering high E on the first violin simulates the high-pitched whistling that so tormented him, while the return of the "fate" motif initiates the sombre conclusion.

The formation of the first professional Russian string quartet in Russia in 1871 was the impetus that prompted both Borodin and Tchaikovsky to tackle a genre that some of their colleagues felt to be too Western. But Borodin was less of a nationalist than many of his contemporaries, and although he used folk material in his work there is little of it in either of his string quartets. The *String Quartet No. 2* was written during the summer of 1881 while Borodin was holidaying in the country. Like Smetana's first quartet, it is a highly personal work but it exudes an overriding sense of contentment. Dedicated to – and largely inspired by – Borodin's wife Ekaterina (herself a highly talented musician), the quartet also reflects Borodin's enthusiasm for the cello (his own instrument), and the first and third movements are essentially dialogues between the cello and first violin. The first, based around a sunny, affable melody that is passed back and forth with a spontaneous ease, is followed by a Scherzo that recalls Mendelssohn in its light and airy sweetness. Much exploited by Hollywood, the third movement Nocturne is an ardent love duet of a vaguely Oriental colouring, whereas there's a Beethoven-inspired rigour to the finale, beginning with the opening question-and-answer exchanges and continuing through some energetic contrapuntal writing.

The Takács Quartet never settle for a safe or conventional reading of a work. This is particularly true of their performance of the Smetana, which has a vibrancy and a degree of personality that is, at times, alarming. The opening should be attention-grabbing but here it is especially so, with an attack from the viola that is penetratingly incisive. When it comes to the Scherzo à la polka, there's a deliberate roughness that gives the sound a slightly inebriated air. There's greater finesse in the Borodin, plus a strong sense of the quartet as a group of equals – most noticeably in the finale, which achieves the perfect balance between individuality and unanimity.

84

Karlheinz Stockhausen / György Kurtág

Gruppen / Grabstein für Stephan; Stele

Berlin Philharmonic; Claudio Abbado (conductor)

Deutsche Grammophon 447 761-2; full price

In the aftermath of World War II, a summer school was set up at Darmstadt near Frankfurt which became the centre of the European avant-garde, a forcing ground of experimentation. Among the most avid seekers of new systems for structuring musical sounds was Karlheinz Stockhausen, who, building on the total serialism of Webern (see p.199), attempted to subject both time and pitch to the same rigorous organizational principles. In *Gruppen* (Groups) these ideas are spectacularly united with a concept of performance as ritualized event.

Gruppen was initially conceived, in 1954, as a work for tape and orchestra, but within three years it had transmuted into a piece for three orchestras, each comprising six woodwind instruments, seven or eight brass, six percussion and sixteen or eighteen strings. The music is underpinned by the perception of rhythm, tempo and pitch as aspects of the same phenomenon – ie, if you slow down any note sufficiently it starts to be heard as a beat. However, it's the spatial dimension of the work that makes the immediate impact, especially in performance. Arrayed on three sides of the audience, and each with its own conductor, the three orchestras merge in accelerations and crescendos, then separate into a three-way conversation in which independent tempos are combined or fragments of sound fly between the groups – as in the work's climax, when a great brass chord swirls around the hall. *Gruppen* is a whirlwind of sounds that often seems bewilderingly arbitrary but possesses a cumulative energy that is ultimately exhilarating.

The Hungarian composer György Kurtág's first contact with the avant-garde was as a student in Paris in the 1950s. But unlike the "objective" approach of Stockhausen and Boulez, Kurtág assimilated his newly acquired techniques into an already extremely idiosyncratic musical language, in which a sense of alienation and human frailty is never far from the surface. In recent years Kurtág has begun to write for large forces, and his preoccupation with mortality has generated an even more personal style, in which the vulnerable voices of small instrumental groups are made all the more acute by being set against a background of grand statements and rich sonorities.

Grabstein für Stephan (Gravestone for Stephan) was written in 1989 as a memorial to a friend. At its centre a solo guitar seems to represent a static, human presence around which groups of instruments are placed like mourners. It opens with the soloist's gentle plucking of open strings (the work's central motif), over which a shifting array of grief-suggesting sounds (low strings, assorted percussion, wailing alarm signals) are layered. *Stele* (1994) employs the orchestra in a more conventional manner, though with a large tuned percussion section which includes pianos, celesta and cimbalon. At times suggestive of Mahler, at others of Bartók, this is intensely sad music: a tentative, ghostly opening movement moves, without a break, into a clamorous lament before culminating in a finale of immense and terrible gravity.

Claudio Abbado, one of the few top-flight conductors to consistently champion the music of the post-war avant-garde, here gives a thrilling reading of *Gruppen*. No CD could adequately convey the experience of being hemmed in by three orchestras, but the engineers have achieved a wonderful illusion of space on this live recording. The two Kurtág pieces are even more impressive: there's a strong sense, in both works, of the different sections of the orchestra functioning like actors in a tragedy. Abbado controls his forces with an unfailing sense of the right emphasis at the right moment to deliver performances of affecting power and simplicity.

85

Johann Strauss the Younger

Waltzes

Vienna Philharmonic; Willi Boskovsky (director)

Decca 443 473-2; 2 CDs; mid-price

The origins of the waltz are a little cloudy, but it probably derives from the Ländler, a similar but slower German dance that's also in triple time (three beats in a bar). By the second half of the eighteenth century, the waltz had become a dance of fashion, especially in Vienna. The fashion had turned into a craze by the 1800s and many commentators began to write disapprovingly of the immorality of a dance that brought the partners into such close and energetic proximity. Charles Burney, the music historian and friend of Mozart (who composed several waltzes), wrote that "having seen it performed by a select party of foreigners, we could not help reflecting how uneasy an English mother would be to see her daughter so familiarly treated, and still more to witness the obliging manner in which the freedom is returned."

Two men dominated the Viennese dance scene in the second quarter of the nineteenth century, feeding the insatiable demand for new music – Josef Lanner and Johann Strauss the Elder. Strauss began his career as the leader of Lanner's orchestra before setting up an outfit that rapidly established itself at the heart of Viennese musical life. Strauss the Elder programmed waltzes into all his concerts and was in huge demand for the city's many balls, the grandest of which took place in the lavish splendour of the Sofiensaal. Johann Strauss had three sons, all of whom wrote waltzes, and one of whom, also

Johann, brought waltz music to a peak of wit, elegance and sophistication.

Johann the Younger wrote his first waltz at the age of six, but was initially thwarted in his desire to be a composer since his father wanted him to work in a bank. In the end he formed his own small orchestra and made his debut a few days before his nineteenth birthday, playing several of his own compositions. He soon won himself a reputation to rival his father's, and when the latter died five years later Johann amalgamated the two orchestras and became the undisputed "Waltz King".

Johann once claimed that he merely took over the waltz form from his father, and indeed the structure of his waltzes is similar to the later works of his elders: slow introduction, a sequence of contrasting tunes and a quick coda. However, Johann the Younger greatly increased the length of the central sections, introduced a greater sense of variety to the melodies, and enhanced the textural complexities to an almost symphonic level – this is what makes his waltzes so satisfying as concert music (and earned the praise of that most exacting of judges, Arnold Schoenberg). He also had an outstanding facility for writing instantly memorable melodies which impart a very specific character to each piece. All are by definition joyful and uplifting but there is subtle difference between the exuberant jollity of *The Blue Danube* and the more ingratiating sweetness of *Liebeslieder*.

You don't have to be the Vienna Philharmonic to play this music, but it certainly helps. On this double CD (featuring fifteen works by Johann the Younger and two by his brother Josef) the orchestra is directed by Willi Boskovsky, who follows the practice of both Johanns by assuming the position of Stehgeiger (standing violinist), playing and directing at the same time. He may lack the drive and the personality of some of the star conductors who regularly dip a toe in this repertoire, but arguably that is to the music's advantage: ensemble is wonderfully tight while the pulse and phrasing of the music has all the requisite sexiness and panache.

86

Richard Strauss

Also sprach Zarathustra; Till Eulenspiegel; Don Juan

Berlin Philharmonic; Herbert von Karajan (conductor)

Deutsche Grammophon 447 441-2; mid-price

Following the example of Berlioz's *Symphonie fantastique* (see p.31), orchestral music that aimed to tell a story or evoke the atmosphere of a particular place became *de rigueur* among the more adventurous Romantic composers. With the orchestral works of Richard Strauss, written in the last years of the nineteenth century, the tone poem reached its highest level of brilliance and sophistication.

Notable for their flamboyant gestures, complicated counterpoint and remarkable melodies, Strauss's tone poems are the descendants of those by Berlioz and Liszt, but their musical stories are even more expansive and dramatic. *Don Juan* (1888) was the first of these works to get Strauss noticed. In less than twenty minutes of music he showed himself to be both a master of his craft and a radical innovator, making demands upon the orchestra (especially the horns) that were more strenuous than those of any previous composer. The piece recounts the loves and losses of the amorous Don Juan, who is characterized throughout the score by a horn call of Wagnerian intensity. Some gushingly exciting string writing leads to a love scene in which the oboe solo prefigures many of the sentimental tunes that were to come in Strauss's operas. The finale, leading to the anti-hero's damnation, is a blazing crescendo of devastating power.

In *Till Eulenspiegels lustige Streiche* (Till Eulenspiegel's Merry Pranks) Strauss wrote an even more concentrated vignette, this time about a comic rogue from German legend who is constantly cocking a snook at authority. Strauss subtitled this work a Rondo because Till's jaunty theme – initially stated on the horn – keeps bouncing back throughout the work. This is Strauss at his most uninhibited, with wonderfully deft instrumental touches detailing Till's various adventures – causing chaos at a market, impersonating a priest – until he is finally caught and hanged.

Strauss's tone poems exude an energy and self-belief which, eventually, could not be contained by short orchestral pieces. In works such as *Also sprach Zarathustra* (Thus spake Zarathustra), he became increasingly ambitious in terms both of length and of its intellectual pretensions. Nietzsche's book of the same name had only been published a few years when Strauss chose, in 1896, to write a tone poem inspired by it. The Nietzschean philosophy of the *Übermensch*, with its denigration of human weakness, appealed to Strauss's overweening sense of his own heroic destiny. His response was a work of enormous dimensions, a free-flowing fantasia which, leaving aside its philosphical aspirations, creates some awe-inspiring orchestral sounds. Not least of these is the work's inspired "sunrise" opening, famously used by Kubrick in his film *2001*. Nothing else quite lives up to this, and, taken as a whole, the work's eight episodes (each with a heading from Nietzsche) tend to meander in all but the most brilliant performances. It's not without touches of lightheartedness, however: "Zarathustra's dance", towards the end of the work, is cast in the form of a Viennese waltz – albeit one with a decidely rustic flavour.

These three works are well suited to Karajan's flamboyance and the Berlin Philharmonic's rich and refulgent tone, and in their 1973 recording both conductor and orchestra hit the mark in thrilling fashion. Karajan takes *Zarathustra* completely seriously, and achieves a quality of sound so rich, but also so incisive, as to overcome the work's bombast and prolixity. What he cannot disguise – indeed he revels in it – is the often brash exhibitionism of Strauss's orchestral writing, an aspect of the music which many people have found unbearably vulgar and even sinister.

87

Richard Strauss

Vier letzte Lieder (Four Last Songs); 12 Orchesterlieder

Elisabeth Schwarzkopf; Berlin Radio Symphony Orchestra / London Symphony Orchestra; George Szell (conductor)

EMI CDM 5 66908-2; mid-price

After the end of World War II, when he was widely condemned for his collaboration with the Nazis, Richard Strauss fell into a deep depression. Encouraged to begin composing again by his son Franz, Strauss started to work on a song setting for soprano and orchestra. In 1947 he had copied a poem by Eichendorff, *Im Abendrot* (At Dusk) into his diary, below a newspaper clipping describing the destruction of Dresden. The poem tells the story of an old couple who, after a lifetime together, look to the sunset and ask "Is this perhaps death?" Its valedictory significance for Strauss was obvious, and by setting it for soprano he was paying tribute to his wife Pauline the inspiration for many of the great soprano roles in his operas. Having completed the setting by the middle of 1948, Strauss turned to the work of a living poet, Hermann Hesse, selecting four poems to add to *Im Abendrot*. In the end he only completed three Hesse settings: *Frühling* (Spring), *Beim Schlafengehen* (Going to Sleep), and *September*.

Published after the composer's death, the *Vier letzte Lieder* (Four Last Songs) are the crowning achievement of a life devoted to composing for the female voice. Each song alludes to death and the passage of time, but the extended flow of melody – so characteristic of Strauss's vocal writing – also makes them seem both life-affirming and celebratory. Of the Hesse settings *Frühling* is, surprisingly, the most turbulent, as Strauss mirrors the text's rapid transition from tombs to blue skies with a heavy, rolling orchestral movement that is transformed into something rhapsodic within a matter of bars. In *September* Hesse's words mourn the ending of summer while Strauss's orchestral writing suggests a shimmering whirl of light and scattering leaves over which the soloist plots an initially steady line that gradually becomes more animated. Only with the short horn solo in the orchestral coda is an autumnal note introduced.

Beim Schlafengehen is essentially a lullaby, a yearning for sleep (and by implication for death) as a realm where the soul can soar "in the magic circle of night". This journey of the soul is expressed through a poignant violin solo after the second verse – the delicate frailty of the violin line making a contrast with the full-throated rapture of the soprano in the final verse. The precise order of the songs was not specified by Strauss, but most singers end the cycle with the elegiac *Im Abendrot*, in which the melancholy of Eichendorff's verses, allied to the soaring pathos of the music, creates a mood of almost unbearable sadness. A great surge of orchestral sound begins the piece and once again the voice enters quietly, subdued in mood with long phrases over a busy orchestral background. Trilling flutes represent the flight of a pair of larks – a motif that is repeated over the dark, sepulchral tones of the song's closing chords.

Strauss's operas and songs provided Elisabeth Schwarzkopf with ideal material for her light, if melancholic, soprano voice. The *Four Last Songs* were premiered by the heavy-weight Wagnerian Kirsten Flagstad, but they are better served by Schwarzkopf's gentle, understated approach, in which the poetry defines the interpretation of the music rather than the other way around. Almost alone among the great interpreters of these songs she performs them as if the words really mattered. George Szell conducts what on paper seems to be a second-division orchestra but which produces some truly ravishing sounds, including an exquisitely vibrant violin solo in *Beim Schlafengehen*.

88

Igor Stravinsky

Petrushka; Le Sacre du printemps

New York Philharmonic / Cleveland Orchestra; Pierre Boulez (conductor)

Sony SMK 64 109; full price

The first night of Stravinsky's ballet *Le Sacre du printemps* (The Rite of Spring) on May 29, 1913, is one of the most notorious events in the history of twentieth-century Western culture. The audience at the Champs-Elysées Theatre in Paris, having sat through three safe ballets, erupted in fury almost as soon as the curtain went up on the new work. The noise reached such levels that the dancers couldn't hear the music and the choreographer, Nijinsky, was forced to stand in the wings shouting instructions at them.

What was it that was so objectionable about the new work? Partly the choreography (Stravinsky later described the female dancers as "a group of knock-kneed and long-braided Lolitas jumping up and down") but more the music itself. By even the most advanced standards of the time, Stravinsky's score was revolutionary, in particular in the way melody and harmony were virtually eradicated and rhythm pushed into the foreground.

The ballet's scenario, worked out by Stravinsky and the designer Nicholas Roerich, depicts the advent of spring in ancient Russia and the sacrifice of a young girl who dances herself to death in front of her tribe. Stravinsky matched this primitivist vision with music of elemental power. After a bleak, writhing introduction, the main action begins with the strings relentlessly pounding out a series of thunderous chords. Stravinsky employs the orchestra almost as a unit of percussion in rhythms that are convulsive and irregular. The melodies that do appear are derived from Russian folk music and their treatment is either fragmentary or else obsessively repetitive. The ballet climaxes in the "Sacrificial Dance", in which the irregularity of the pulse creates a propulsive, nervous energy that is terrifying to listen to and extraordinarily difficult to play.

Stravinsky had begun working for Diaghilev's Russian Ballet company in 1909 as a brilliant orchestral colourist in the mould of his teacher Rimsky-Korsakov. Two years later, with his third ballet, *Petrushka*, he forged his own sharper and more brilliant musical identity. The work began as a piece for piano and orchestra but Diaghilev persuaded Stravinsky to extend it into a full-length ballet. The story is set at a Shrovetide fair. An old magician brings his three puppets – a ballerina, a Moor, and the clown Petrushka – to life. Petrushka loves the ballerina but she despises him and flirts with the Moor, who then kills the jealous Petrushka. The magician shows the horrified crowd that Petrushka is just a puppet but his spirit mocks them all from the rooftops. This is one of Stravinsky's most colourful scores, which in its vivid polytonality (the use of different keys at the same time) and its dynamic rhythms put a modern slant on the Russian Ballet's trademark exoticism. Ballets are often episodic, but Stravinsky replaces the idea of a sequence of discrete "numbers" with a pulsating collage of overlapping sounds and melodies (many of them borrowed) that brilliantly evokes the bustle of the crowd and the skewed private worlds of the puppets.

Pierre Boulez brings the same qualities to conducting as he does to composing – a scrupulous objectivity that often seems unconcerned with the emotional dimensions of a work. If that sounds unpromising, then this 1969 recording of *Le Sacre du printemps* shows that such an approach can generate high levels of excitement – this is a performance of great power and an inexorable sense of momentum. In *Petrushka*, Boulez's other great strength, his ability to create textural transparency, is very much in evidence. This may not be the most atmospheric performance, but it reveals the primary colours of Stravinsky's score with an unrivalled clarity.

89

Igor Stravinsky

Pulcinella; Renard; Octet; Ragtime

London Sinfonietta; Esa-Pekka Salonen (conductor)

Sony SK 45 965; full price

In 1920 Sergei Diaghilev asked Stravinsky to orchestrate some pieces by the eighteenth-century composer Pergolesi (see p.121) for a ballet about the *commedia dell'arte* character Pulcinella. Though initially sceptical, Stravinsky "fell in love" with Pergolesi's music, but his subsequent arrangements were far from the soft-centred concoctions that Diaghilev had intended. Employing a small chamber orchestra and three singers, Stravinsky retained Pergolesi's melodies and bass lines but stamped his own mark on the music with unusual orchestration (one piece is for double-bass and trombone), spiky dissonances and unpredictable rhythmic accents. Like Picasso's designs for *Pulcinella*, Stravinsky's Pergolesi arrangements are not so much pastiche as the affectionate re-fashioning of one period in terms of another.

Pulcinella pushed Stravinsky into a radical re-appraisal of the forms of Baroque and Classical music which was to provide the inspiration for his own compositional style for the next thirty years. Neo-classicism, as this style became known, was a reaction against the excess and subjectivity of late Romanticism, replacing it with something ordered and precise. Textures were light and clear, which in Stravinsky's case meant an emphasis on woodwind rather than strings. Neo-classicism could also be playful in its treatment of tradition, and it provided a witty alternative to the more severe and high-minded avant-garde music of Schoenberg, Berg and Webern.

Written in 1922, the *Octet* for wind instruments is the first piece in which Stravinsky completely embraced neo-classicism. Counterpoint and rhythmic propulsion are very much to the fore, though the inspiration seems more Bach than Mozart. Stravinsky claimed that the idea for the instrumentation came to him in a dream; whatever its origins, the combination of two trumpets, two trombones, two bassoons, a flute and a clarinet makes for a wonderfully lucid texture which, in Stravinsky's own words, "renders more evident the musical architecture". Objectivity was the point of the exercise and Stravinsky was adamant that the *Octet* was "not an 'emotive' work but a musical composition based on objective elements which are sufficient in themselves." All of which makes it sound rather dry, which the *Octet* isn't. As in many of his neo-classical works, there's an element of witty subversion, from the over-insistent bassoon ostinato (a persistently repeated figure) that seems a foretaste of Minimalism, to the syncopated coda in the finale with its heavy-footed but light hearted rumba.

In 1918, six years before jazz became an influence for many classical composers, Stravinsky discovered ragtime (while living in Switzerland) – not through hearing it but by seeing it in printed form. He wrote several ragtime-inspired works, including the four-minute *Ragtime* for eleven instruments grouped around what he called the "bordello-piano sonority" of the Hungarian dulcimer or cimbalom. Once again Stravinsky's amazing capacity for assimilation is revealed – there's an effortless grasp of the dance's rhythmic character which is given a bizarre twist through the curiously mechanistic instrumentation and the unpredictable lurch of the internal rhythms.

Stravinsky seems to have favoured objective performances of his music: "I have often said that my music is to be 'read', to be 'executed', but not to be 'interpreted'." Salonen conforms to this principle by working for a degree of transparency that allows the energy of the counterpoint to emerge with a diagrammatic clarity. It's an aim he achieves, and the result has an amazing presence. He's greatly helped by an ensemble of virtuosic instrumentalists and exceptionally vivid engineering. These may be cool performances, but the music is too vivacious for them ever to be cold.

90

Igor Stravinsky

Symphony of Psalms; Symphony in C; Symphony in Three Movements

London Symphony Orchestra; Michael Tilson Thomas (conductor)

Sony SK 53275; full price

The fact that Stravinsky used traditional titles for many of his works reveals a fascination with the past but not a slavish adherence to it. Tradition was a living thing for Stravinsky, who felt that existing forms could be re-fashioned and manipulated in whatever way a composer chose. He wrote no fewer than five works with the word "symphony" in the title, but in each one he approached the concept of the large-scale work in a radically different way.

Stravinsky was a quietly devout man who had long wanted to compose a major religious work. Commissioned by Serge Koussevitsky in 1930 to write something for the fiftieth anniversary of the Boston Symphony Orchestra, he decided on a three-part choral setting using verses from Psalms 38 and 39, and all of Psalm 150. He set the text in Latin, to give the words a universal quality, and stripped the orchestra of its violins, violas and clarinets, adding two pianos. His intention was "to counter the many composers who had abused these magisterial verses as pegs for their own lyrico-sentimental 'feelings'."

The result is austerely ritualistic and immensely powerful. The first section, "Exaudi orationem meam" (Hear my prayer), sets the dry, animated sounds of wind instruments and piano against the supplicatory chanting of the chorus. Bach is the referent for the second section, in which two fugues are combined – the first, by the orchestra, is stark and angular, the second, by the chorus, solid and expansive. Their combination creates the same desperate impact as a chorus in a Bach *Passion*, despite the many biting dissonances. The final section is a psalm of praise which contains several references to specific musical instruments but which Stravinsky, with his characteristic avoidance of the obvious, refuses to "illustrate". It is extremely beautiful, but it's a chaste beauty based on the simplicity of repeated phrases, such as the gentle "Alleluia" that occurs three times, or the phrase "Laudate Dominum", with its rhythm like a muttered prayer.

Eight years later another commission, this time from the Chicago Symphony Orchestra, resulted in the *Symphony in C*, a more obvious orchestral showpiece. It's a work that shows Stravinsky's great capacity for synthesis. There are clear formal and thematic references to other works – in the first two movements an unlikely mélange of Beethoven, Haydn and Tchaikovsky – but the whole work has a typically Stravinskian acerbity, with crisp woodwind writing, bustling counterpoint, and heavily accented motor rhythms.

The third of Stravinsky's three "American" symphonies, the *Symphony in Three Movements*, is a very different kind of work. Completing it in 1945, Stravinsky described it as his "War Symphony" and its outer movements have a stridency and an edge that generates a sense of anxiety and links the work to the aggressive sound-world of *Le Sacre du printemps*. On the other hand the slow movement, in which the harp plays a prominent part, looks forward to the elegant refinement of his opera *The Rake's Progress*.

Michael Tilson Thomas is one of the most dynamic of recent Stravinsky conductors. Though always receptive to the music's brightness and rhythmic spring, he also brings an unusual degree of warmth and bloom to the orchestral sound. In the *Symphony of Psalms* the right balance between chorus and orchestra is difficult to achieve, but Thomas manages it just about perfectly, while also introducing an element of dramatic tension into the music that increases its devotional focus, above all in the last section. In the other two "American" symphonies, there's a flair and an excitement to the orchestral playing that is completely engaging.

91

Tylman Susato and others

Dances from "Danserye" and other pieces

The Early Music Consort of London / The Morley Consort; David Munrow (director)

Testament SBT 1080; full price

From the late 1960s to the middle 1970s, the world of Renaissance and medieval music was transformed by the charismatic figure of David Munrow. A brilliant recorder player and an inspirational communicator, he generated enormous enthusiasm for what had been thought of as a rather esoteric area of music. With his group the Early Music Ensemble he produced a number of highly successful TV and radio programmes, as well as several recordings. This disc combines two recordings dedicated to sixteenth-century dance music.

A huge number of different dance forms existed in Renaissance Europe, many of which were spread across the continent by itinerant dancers and acrobats. As with a jazz band, the musicians improvised and made their own arrangements of tunes rather than playing from the page. With the advent of printing, however, collections of dance music began to appear throughout the sixteenth century, primarily for the benefit of amateur musicians.

One hugely popular collection was *Danserye*, published in 1551 by the Antwerp musician and printer Tylman Susato from his shop "at the sign of the crumhorn", which went through 27 editions over the next hundred years. *Danserye* is an anthology of already existing dances and songs in non-vocal arrangements made by Susato: most of the music was the equivalent of pop songs but it also contained more sophisticated pieces by composers like Josquin Desprez (see p.59). It's an enormously varied collection that includes grand processional music like the stately *Pavane La Bataille* as well as extremely lively pieces like the *Ronde and Salterelle*. Instrumentation is not specified, so the joy for an interpreter is choosing instruments to suit the character of a piece. Munrow favours a theatrical approach and his arrangements exploit, wherever possible, the rich variety of instrumental colour available to him. So, for example, the thick mix of cornett, crumhorn, dulcian and sackbut (all dark-toned wind instruments) in *Ronde mon amy* is followed by the smooth sound of a group of viols (bowed instruments) in *Allemaigne and Recoupe*.

His selection of Italian instrumental music from slightly later in the century centres on the work of Giorgio Mainerio, whose *Il primo libro de balli a quattro voci* (First Book of Dances in Four Parts) of 1578 is one of the few Italian dance collections of the period. This is more folkish and less courtly sounding music than *Danserye*. Choice of instruments is, again, highly colourful. In one dance, *Ballo francese*, the melody is played on the xylophone, while several others feature the distinctly Italian sound of the mandolin. In both these collections Munrow's bold attack and emphasis on rhythmic drive means that the music truly sounds as if it should be danced to.

That cannot be said for the last collection on the disc, Thomas Morley's dances from *The First Booke of Consort Lessons* of 1599, which was clearly conceived as recreational chamber music for amateurs. Like Susato's *Danserye*, these aren't original compositions but arrangements of popular music. Unlike Susato, though, Morley names his sources (mainly English composers) and specifies the instruments – various combinations of treble lute, pandora and cittern (all plucked stringed instruments), bass viol, treble viol and flute. The result is more reposeful and frequently melancholic music, in which the lutenist (the uncredited James Tyler) has the most virtuosic role. As can be said for many Munrow performances, there have probably been more technically sophisticated accounts of this music in the last twenty years (often by artists inspired by his example) but few convey the same level of enjoyment and spontaneity.

92

Pyotr Il'yich Tchaikovsky

Suites from Swan Lake, The Sleeping Beauty and The Nutcracker

Berlin Philharmonic Orchestra; Mstislav Rostropovich (conductor)

Deutsche Grammophon 449 726-2; mid-price

The charm and elegance of Tchaikovsky's three ballets (*Swan Lake*, *The Sleeping Beauty* and *The Nutcracker*) represent the other side of a composer better known for his dark and melancholy view of life, but they met with little more than polite approval during his lifetime – in sharp contrast to the tortured final symphonies, which were instant and lasting successes.

Commissioned by the Imperial Theatre to write his first ballet in 1875, Tchaikovsky gladly accepted the challenge, partly because of his poor financial situation, and partly because, as he wrote to Rimsky-Korsakov, "I have long had the wish to try my hand at this kind of music." As with his symphonies, he had little by way of native precedent, since most earlier Russian ballet scores were nothing but vapid background music. *Swan Lake*, however, is made up of extended quasi-symphonic movements, unified by recurring themes that conjure up a kaleidoscopic range of moods and feelings. Its initial haunting oboe melody over gentle harp background becomes more and more impassioned, but no less typical is the exhilarating waltz that follows or the daintily comic tripping of the ensuing Cygnets' theme.

Thirteen years passed before Tchaikovsky returned to ballet, midway between his fifth and sixth symphonies. Their influence is discernible in *The Sleeping Beauty*'s remarkable seamlessness and inventive colouring, although at the time the score was criticized for being "too symphonic". This time Tchaikovsky collaborated closely with the choreographer Petipa who guided him, section by section, through the work's composition. Elaborately constructed, the ballet contains movements within movements which are, effectively, miniature concertos for the orchestral section leaders. Like *Swan Lake*, *The Sleeping Beauty* abounds in the most expansive melodies, the most notable being the great Adagio that builds its sweeping melody to a rapturous climax, and the glorious *Valse (No. 4)* that out-Strausses Johann Strauss and brings the work to a thrilling close.

For his last ballet, completed just before his death, Tchaikovsky turned to a version by the elder Dumas of an E.T.A. Hoffmann tale, *The Nutcracker and the Mouse King*, in which a little girl's dreams on Christmas Night bring her toys to life. The juxtaposition of extremes – fusing episodes of exotic rhythm, barbaric vitality and tonal brilliance to scenes of gentle, almost whispered beauty – is breathtaking. The score is celebrated for its "Dance of the Sugar Plum Fairy", in which the composer became the first to use the recently invented celesta in an orchestra, but more remarkable are the rush of the "Trepak" (Russian Dance), the languorous and dreamy "Arab Dance" and the glittering exoticism of the "Chinese Dance". The ballet's crowning achievement is its final number, the "Waltz of the Flowers". Above a waltz rhythm of captivating elegance Tchaikovsky spins a simple thread of melody that develops into an unstoppable surge that is carried headlong into the final, tremendous chords.

Mstislav Rostropovich is a finer cellist than he is a conductor, but in the right repertoire his sheer pleasure in music-making can yield tremendous results. Tchaikovsky is one of his calling cards and these full-blooded performances of the ballet suites (reductions of the full-length works to their highlights) are animated by the conviction of a true believer. Every bar of the music is delivered with an overpowering sincerity that avoids the sentimentality into which, with some interpreters, this music oftens descends. The Berlin Philharmonic is in muscular but highly responsive form: like Rostropovich the orchestra seems to enjoy every minute of the music, and the sound is warmly balanced and richly recorded.

93

Pyotr Il'yich Tchaikovsky / Sergei Rachmaninov

Piano Concerto No. 1 / Piano Concerto No. 3

Martha Argerich (piano); Bavarian Radio Symphony Orchestra / RSO Berlin; Kirill Kondrashin / Riccardo Chailly (conductor)

Philips 446 673-2; full price

Tchaikovsky's *Piano Concerto No. 1*, like several of his works, had a pretty disastrous start. On Christmas Eve, 1874, Tchaikovsky played it to Russia's leading pianist, Nikolai Rubinstein (the intended dedicatee), who pronounced it unplayable and hardly worth revising. An affronted Tchaikovsky re-dedicated the work to Hans von Bülow, who gave its triumphant premiere in Boston nearly a year later. To be fair to Rubinstein, he soon changed his mind about the work, and important changes were made to it, most notably to the famous opening. Alexander Siloti, who helped arrange the score for its third edition, suggested that the repeated chords of Tchaikovsky's original be replaced by piano chords covering the whole of the instrument's range; Tchaikovsky agreed, thereby creating one of classical music's great attention grabbing effects.

The first movement is by far the longest and thematically the richest, with its lilting second main theme being subjected to some wonderfully imaginative transformations. The slow movement begins with pizzicato strings over which a solo flute plays the gentlest of lullabies, which is then taken over by the piano. What's novel about this movement is the way Tchaikovsky inserts a skittish Scherzo into its centre before the original lullaby theme recurs, this time with the piano weaving a delicate ornamental descant over the top of it. The finale seems about to follow the pattern of a conventional last movement, with a sharply accented folk melody as the main theme, but a broader luxuriant melody enters and the two function in tandem until the final bars reach a thunderous climax, as the pianist lets fly with the most astonishingly difficult octave runs in both hands.

Rachmaninov, who was twenty when Tchaikovsky died, studied composition with Taneyev (who gave the Russian premiere of Tchaikovsky's concerto), and the piano with Zverev, who also taught Siloti – Rachmaninov's cousin. Not surprisingly Rachmaninov saw himself as the successor of his great Russian forebears, and his *Piano Concerto No. 3* stands as the apotheosis of the Romantic concerto. Indebted to Tchaikovsky for its emotional rush and to Liszt for its virtuosity, it was written in 1909 as a vehicle for Rachmaninov's own brilliant piano playing and received its first performance in New York the following year.

This immense, symphonic concerto is also one of the most difficult, though the chant-like opening theme suggests otherwise. In this work Rachmaninov overcame his habit of signposting the introduction of new material by bringing the music to a halt, and his subtle metamorphosis of the first movement's theme into a leit-motif for the whole work creates a continuity unprecedented in his work. The slow movement is essential Rachmaninov: a melancholy theme that develops along rhapsodic lines, with the orchestral and the piano writing textured very thickly. Even by Rachmaninov's standards the finale is overloaded with material, but in the hands of a virtuoso it can sound richly opulent and extremely exciting.

There are many recordings of the Tchaikovsky concerto, but two artists dominate the field – Vladimir Horowitz and Martha Argerich. Both have recorded it several times and each performance has its own special insights. This 1980 live performance by Argerich is marked by a tumultuous drive – there's a feeling of the notes just tumbling out, but they're guided by a restless intelligence which is capable of making the music seem freshly written. Similarly in the Rachmaninov, also recorded live, there is a vibrant and unpredictable edge to the playing that imparts a sense of discovery and breathes life into the more prolix moments.

94

Pyotr Il'yich Tchaikovsky

Symphonies Nos. 4, 5 and 6

London Symphony Orchestra; Igor Markevitch (conductor)

Philips 438 335-2; 2 CDs; mid-price

Whereas Brahms struggled under the weight of Beethoven's example before finally getting round to writing his first symphony in 1876, Tchaikovsky faced the opposite problem – he had to create his own precedent. The three symphonies Tchaikovsky completed between 1866 and 1875 frequently betray the fact that Russia had no symphonic tradition of its own, but with the masterful *Symphony No. 4* his apprenticeship was clearly over.

Tchaikovsky viewed the symphony as the vessel for his most profound thoughts and feelings, and extreme emotional turmoil accompanied the composition of each of them. The writing of *Symphony No. 4* was interrupted by the breakdown of his ill-advised marriage (a desperate attempt to screen his homosexuality) and a half-hearted suicide attempt, and the music is marked by a sense of dejection and introspection carried to extremes – particularly in the first movement, which begins with a dramatic fanfare representing "Fate". The writing is consistently inventive, with rich instrumental colours, blazing fanfares and some implicit humour in the syncopated third-movement Scherzo, but it is the charging, ebullient finale that justifies the use of superlatives – incorporating variations on a Russian folk song, this is the composer's most exciting symphonic invention, ending in a torrent of enthusiasm after the violent incursions of the "Fate" motif.

Of his *Symphony No. 5*, written eleven years later, Tchaikovsky wrote: "I have become convinced that the symphony is unsuccessful. There is something repellent about it . . . it is all most distressing." If this is distressing work, it is because of its unguarded candour rather than any musical failings. Given over to an excessive melancholy, it veers between the depths of despair and a series of emotional climaxes bordering on the hysterical. Dominated by another "Fate" motif, the work hinges on a slow movement of extraordinary, song-filled beauty before ending, like the fourth, on a defiant note – although there is a suggestion throughout this pugilistic episode of the composer putting a brave face on things.

The sixth and last of his symphonies, subtitled *The Pathétique*, is one of the most over-wrought ever written. Tchaikovsky loved it, and wrote to friends with joyful news of its completion; six months later, in 1893, he killed himself. The work's sub-title was added by the composer's brother, and seems entirely appropriate for a work that, despite its striking beauty, can sound weighed down by self-pity. Although the opening movement contains one of Tchaikovsky's loveliest themes, a sense of intense internal struggle is conveyed by extremes of dynamics – indeed, no previous symphony had displayed such violent ranges between soft and loud. The second movement is a ghostly piece written in a rhythm that seems to be imitating a waltz but never quite becomes one. In the third movement a hectic march takes over, but any hints of triumph are soon dispelled. Unusually the symphony ends with a slow movement, and it's the most anguished music Tchaikovsky ever composed – the emotional weight of this Adagio (marked "lamentoso") becomes ever more burdensome until, breaking down with grief, the music disappears into the darkness from which it emerged.

Few conductors have been able to resist the pull of Tchaikovsky's last three symphonies; fewer still have been able to do them justice. The chief requirement of any conductor performing these symphonies is discipline, and Igor Markevitch, a Czech conductor prominent during the 1960s, when these recordings were made, was famed for the lack of indulgence with which he conducted late-Romantic music. There isn't a sentimental or poorly judged note in any of these performances, and the London Symphony Orchestra play with equal measures of fire and precision.

95

Michael Tippett

A Child of Our Time

Faye Robinson (soprano); Sarah Walker (mezzo-soprano); Jon Garrison (tenor); John Cheek (bass); City of Birmingham Symphony Orchestra and Chorus; Michael Tippett (conductor)

Collins 13392; full price

Michael Tippett was one of the most widely read and intellectually curious of modern composers, and his spiritual and political beliefs play a conspicuous part in much of his work. In the 1930s he underwent Jungian analysis and this had the most profound and far-reaching effect on his music. Much of his work represents a quest for wholeness, a reconciliation of the dark and the light he believed to be within everyone. A committed pacifist, he had a spell in Wormwood Scrubs during World War II for refusing to carry out his non-combatant military duties.

Tippett began his oratorio *A Child of Our Time* at the beginning of the war, and it was given its first performance in 1944. During the Depression years he had been profoundly affected by the social deprivation caused by unemployment, but it was the 1938 Nazi pogrom known as Kristallnacht that was the work's real catalyst. The Nazis' justification for the pogrom was the assassination in Paris of a German diplomat by a young Polish Jew, Herschel Grynszpan. The figure of Grynszpan – the disaffected, suffering outcast – became the symbolic protagonist of Tippett's work. Tippett originally asked T.S. Eliot to write the libretto but when Eliot saw the scenario he felt that any contribution that he made would be distractingly poetic. Tippett duly wrote his own text, one that was simple in diction although complex in its symbolism. Modelled on Handel's *Messiah* and the Bach Passions in its use of recitatives, arias and choruses, *A Child of Our Time* is divided into three parts: the first conveys a world in winter, held in the grip of oppression; the second tells of the desperation that drives the young man to violence; the third tells of the striving for renewal and wholeness. The most telling line – "I would know my shadow and my light, so shall I at last be whole" – stands as a kind of encapsulation of Tippett's beliefs.

Musically, Tippett was an individualist with an idiosyncratic perspective on tradition. *A Child of Our Time* is sparely orchestrated but it nevertheless imparts a fullness and warmth in which Tippett's enthusiasm for English Renaissance music, Baroque counterpoint and even folk music can be heard. There are four soloists: the alto and bass act for the most part as commentators, while the tenor and soprano have more impassioned and individualized roles. Tippett's most inspired decision, however, was to punctuate the proceedings with five Negro spirituals, at the conclusion of each section, as a counterpart to the Lutheran chorales Bach uses in his Passions. As with Bach's chorales, the effect of hearing familiar, simple communal singing in the context of a dramatic work is profoundly consoling. Tippett's modern but discreet harmonization of the spirituals is never sentimental, and in "Go Down Moses" and the concluding "Deep River" the impact is overwhelming.

A Child of Our Time has proved one of the most popular of all Tippett's works and there are now six recordings of it in the catalogue. Tippett's own, conducted when he was 85, has the advantage of a straightforward directness and sincerity. His four soloists are excellent without being attention-seeking: in particular Faye Robinson's richly incisive voice floats above the chorus in the first spiritual, "Steal Away", with an unforced radiance. Collins' studio recording has a sufficiently spacious sound to create the ambience of a live performance. Although the label ceased making new recordings in 1998, the back catalogue – including this disc – is still readily available.

96

Mark-Anthony Turnage

Your Rockaby; Night Dances; Dispelling the Fears

Martin Robertson (saxophone); Håkan Hardenberger / John Wallace (trumpets); BBC Symphony Orchestra / London Sinfonietta / Philharmonia Orchestra; Andrew Davis / Oliver Knussen / Daniel Harding (conductors)

Argo 452 598-2 (full price)

Mark-Anthony Turnage exploded into prominence in 1988 with the premiere of his opera *Greek*, a brutish vision of Thatcher's Britain that re-located the Oedipus myth to the East End of London. *Greek* was attacked for being crude, strident and simplistic, but even those who disliked it were impressed by the brilliance of the orchestral writing – a powerful mélange of smouldering colours and dark intensity which could pinpoint a mood or an emotion with more directness than the work's rather relentless vocal style.

Turnage began composition lessons with Oliver Knussen at the age of 15. A scholarship led to further study with Gunther Schuller and Hans Werner Henze, but a more profound influence on the evolution of his style was his discovery of jazz. Increasingly his orchestral scores seemed to occupy the same emotional terrain as the work of artists like Gil Evans and Miles Davis, and it is clear that Turnage regards the "visceral quality" and formal freedom of jazz as better able to communicate the anxieties and ambiguities of modern urban life than the formulaic language of classic Modernism.

Night Dances (1981), the first orchestral piece to get Turnage noticed, already displays many typical stylistic touches. Written "to evoke feelings and emotions aroused by my first encounter with Black music", this is an overwhelmingly atmospheric work in four sections that employs a highly original mesh of instrumental voices — shimmering percussion, an amplified solo group, and off-stage string quintet — that manages to be both sensual and unnerving in its restlessness.

Time and again the raw and anguished eloquence of the saxophone — an instrument with which he strongly identifies — figures strongly in Turnage's work and in 1994 he wrote what is, in effect, a saxophone concerto entitled *Your Rockaby* for the saxophonist Martin Robertson. Partly inspired by a Samuel Beckett monologue of the same name, *Your Rockaby* pitches the solitary, keening voice of the saxophone against a kaleidoscopic orchestral backdrop which is part Ravel, part urban sleaze. There's a definite whiff of *film noir* to this work, especially in the edgy central section where the soloist seems to be picking his way through a bewildering and often hostile environment.

The inspiration for *Dispelling the Fears* was a painting by the Australian artist Heather Betts, in which a small area of white is set in a field of enveloping darkness. The painting was a starting point for a twenty-minute concerto for two trumpets that gradually moves from harsh insistency to lyrical rapture. There's an elemental feel to the introduction, and the two trumpets initially seem to circle around each other warily. In fact there is something of a sibling relationship to the solo parts throughout — a closeness with a competitive edge as they swoop around each other, moving together and frequently clashing. It conjures up a bleak, unyielding landscape but in the last third of the work this opens out into a bluesy atmosphere that is less fractured and more subdued.

The first disc to be released by Argo following the company's exclusive contract with Turnage is absolutely stunning, combining lucid sound with warmth and naturalness — despite being performed by different ensembles in different locations. This music is sometimes uncomfortably bleak but the performances are well and truly lived-in, and the soloists bring a degree of finesse and nuance which raise both *Your Rockaby* and *Dispelling the Fears* to a very high level of achievement.

97

Giuseppe Verdi

Messa da Requiem

Cheryl Studer (soprano); Dolora Zajic (mezzo-soprano); Luciano Pavarotti (tenor); Samuel Ramey (bass); Chorus and Orchestra of La Scala, Milan; Riccardo Muti (conductor)

EMI CDS 7 49390-2; 2 CDs; full price

The quality of liturgical music declined during the second half of the nineteenth century, partly as a result of the gradual secularization of Western society but also because the traditions of church music had ossified into something dry and academic. However, several composers were drawn to the Requiem Mass as a type of religious music that could be adapted to an essentially humanistic world-view. Both Brahms and Verdi – who wrote two of the finest Requiems – were profoundly uncertain of the depth of their respective faiths.

The sixty-year-old Verdi was moved to begin his *Messa da Requiem* by the death of the poet and novelist Alessandro Manzoni, whose novel *I promessi sposi* (The Betrothed) had immense patriotic significance for Italians during the campaign for Italian unity. Verdi completed the score just in time for the heavily publicized first performance in 1874, which he conducted at the Church of San Marco in Milan – Manzoni's home city – with a quartet of operatic stars, three of whom had recently performed in his recently completed Egyptian spectacular *Aida*.

Verdi's choice of soloists is indicative of his *Requiem*'s high theatricality. The conductor Hans von Bülow sneeringly dismissed it as Verdi's "latest opera in theatrical vestments", and there is little doubt that this is a Mass that has as much fire and brimstone as it does compassion and consolation. Ignoring the prevailing idioms of Catholic usage, Verdi fell back on what he knew best, creating a score of wild extremes, emotive ensembles and quasi-operatic solos. Much of the orchestration recalls *Aida*, and the origin of at least one of the numbers (the Lacrymosa) is now known to be a discarded duet from his vast historical opera, *Don Carlo*. The work's most dramatic sequence is the extended Dies irae, in which Verdi conjured hair-raising visions of the Last Judgement, using the huge chorus and mighty percussion section to thrilling effect, above all in the opening bars. Verdi added to the impact by scoring a series of fanfares for widely spaced ensembles, grouped in fours (an idea borrowed from Berlioz's *Messe des Morts*) and while this is inevitably more effective live, the effect can still be heart-stopping on disc.

Each of the soloists (soprano, mezzo-soprano, tenor, bass) makes a sizeable contribution to the ninety-minute score, nowhere more poignantly than in the tenor's "Ingemisco tamquam reus" (I groan as one guilty), an aria of the most searing intensity at the end of the Dies irae. Equally hypnotic is the Offertorio, where all four soloists combine in a section that begins serenely before building to a climax of fervent supplication. But not all of the *Requiem* is elaborate: one of the most moving sections, the Agnus Dei, begins with the two female soloists singing quasi-plainchant an octave apart, and this episode's development maintains the spirit of its simple opening.

The most famous recording of this epic work was conducted by Verdi's friend Arturo Toscanini, an electrifying account that pushed the histrionic aspects a little unrelentingly. Riccardo Muti's live recording, made at La Scala in 1987, has the same high-octane intensity (especially in the Dies irae) but is balanced by moments of greater repose. The atmosphere of the event has been superbly caught by the engineers, and the quartet of soloists give near-faultless performances. If Pavarotti's tenor lacks the freshness of youth, he more than compensates by his mature and considered approach, and his contribution to the ensembles is beautifully judged. Zajic and Ramey give relatively subdued performances, but Studer swoops through her music with a relish that is irresistible.

98

Tomás Luis de Victoria

Officium Defunctorum

Magnificat; Philip Cave (director)

Linn Records CKD060; full price

On March 18 and 19, 1603, the funeral of the Dowager Empress Maria of Austria took place at the Madrid convent in which she had lived for the last 22 years of her life. As she was the sister of King Philip II of Spain, her death was commemorated in the most lavish of ceremonies which was repeated a month later in the chapel of the Imperial College. On both occasions music was specially written by Maria's music director and chaplain Tomás Luis de Victoria (1548–1611), music that has come to be regarded as the last great example of Renaissance polyphony.

Victoria was born at Ávila, where he later served as a chorister at the cathedral and attended the Jesuit school of San Gil. Around 1565 he went to Rome to study at another Jesuit institution, the Collegium Germanicum, where he is thought to have come into contact with Palestrina – then the greatest composer of sacred music in Rome. Palestrina may have given him lessons, but whatever Victoria gained from his older colleague, the differences in their respective styles is revealing. Whereas the music of Palestrina creates a mood of serene repose, Victoria transforms the polyphonic technique into a vehicle for fervent and passionate feelings that suggest a more personal relationship with God. Some have discerned the source of this fervour in a particularly Spanish form of Catholicism, an intense piety that is also evident in the writings of the mystic St Teresa of Ávila, and in the visionary paintings of El Greco, both of whom were contemporaries of Victoria.

The music Victoria wrote for the Office of the Dead (Officium Defuntorum) begins with the second lesson of Matins, "Taedet animam meam" (My soul is weary), performed on the first day of the obsequies. It is followed by a setting of the Requiem Mass, performed on the second day, then a funeral motet, "Versa est in luctum", which leads into the climactic service of Absolution, the music building in intensity all the time. "Taedet animam meam" establishes the mood with solemn and austere music, but the Requiem Mass itself is far richer, the opening Requiem aeternam hinting at spiritual aspiration through the slowly swelling chords of its opening. This rising figure is repeated in the Kyrie, but in the short Christe the six-part texture (two sopranos, alto, two tenors and a bass) suddenly gives way to just the four upper voices in a passage of great delicacy. As in Josquin's *Missa Pange Lingua* (see p.59), unity is provided between the different sections by a plainsong *cantus firmus*, or fixed melody, which is mostly sung by the second soprano part. The music culminates in the long Libera me in which the word setting is especially acute. At this point the assembled dignitaries, dressed in black, gathered around the catafalque which was sprinkled with holy water and had incense wafted over it.

Victoria's masterpiece has had several fine recordings – what's special about this one is its sonic purity. Light but incisive women's voices are used for the two upper parts (only male singers would have been used originally) and all the voices combine with an airy transparency in a resonant but warm acoustic. The performance is expressive without ever being forced, changes of mood in the different sections of the Libera me are conveyed through subtle, rather than dramatic, changes of dynamics. A sense of the original liturgical context is provided by appropriate plainsong, which is here sung in a manner that makes it sound of a piece with the polyphony.

99

Antonio Vivaldi

The Four Seasons

Nils-Erik Sparf (violin); The Drottningholm Baroque Ensemble

BIS CD-275; full price

Nearly three centuries after it was composed, *The Four Seasons* of Antonio Vivaldi (1678–1741) continues to be the most popular piece of classical music ever written. It's an astonishing cultural phenomenon which has been largely generated by the recording industry: more than 150 recordings have been made since the first, on the Italian label Cetra, in 1942, and ninety of these are currently in the catalogue. But if *The Four Seasons* has become a self-perpetuating musical cliché, a sure-fire money-spinner for record companies, violin whizz-kids and advertisers alike, it is still a masterpiece. One of the earliest and most successful attempts to depict nature in musical terms, each section is brilliantly inventive, conjuring up markedly contrasted moods and images with a range of vivid and sometimes strange sounds that are beguiling even after repeated listenings.

Born and brought up in Venice, Vivaldi was himself an excellent violinist who learnt the instrument from his father. Though ordained a priest in his early twenties, Vivaldi was to earn his living as a musician working for much of his life at an orphanage for abandoned girls, the Ospedale della Pietà, where the musical standards were of the highest order. But it was actually for one of his many aristocratic patrons, Count Wenzel von Morzin, that he wrote the twelve three-movement violin concertos collectively entitled *Il cimento dell'armonia e dell'inventione* (The Trial of Harmony and Invention). Of these, the first four make up *I quattro stagioni*, or *The Four Seasons*.

When the set was published in 1725, *The Four Seasons* were accompanied by four rather bad sonnets, probably written by Vivaldi himself, with indications as to which lines corresponded to the music. Although it isn't necessary to follow the poems in order to enjoy the music, they do help to shed light on some of the work's more mysterious moments, and most recordings print them with the sleeve-notes. Interestingly Vivaldi's musical depiction of the seasons mixes conventional images with highly original ones: thus Spring's exquisite central movement has an air of wistfulness achieved through a combination of the plaintive violin solo and the gentle murmuring of the rest of the string orchestra, indicating the wind rustling through the trees. Vivaldi's master-stroke here is to undermine the prevailing tranquillity through a rasping two-note figure in the violas, conveying the insistent barking of a dog.

The Four Seasons abounds in such imaginative details: the spooky restlessness of Autumn's central movement, for instance, or the even more disturbing icy dissonances of Winter's opening. And even though the same elements sometimes recur in different seasons (stormy weather, birdsong, people dancing), they are always treated in a completely new way – Summer's last movement storm is positively demonic when compared with its first rumblings in the opening movement.

Despite the availability of so many recordings, there's a handful of performances that have pushed themselves to the top of the pile and this is certainly one of them. Made in 1981, it wasn't the first recording to use original rather than modern instruments but its uncompromising boldness and febrile energy made a really strong impact. There's a rawness to the playing and a sense of uninhibitedness that is absolutely infectious, particularly in the hard-driven faster moments – this is a vision of seasonal change that stresses the elemental more than most. Soloist Nils-Erik Sparf really sets the pace with an almost improvisatory flair, but he's equally strong in the more lyrical passages, treating Vivaldi's insinuating melodies as if they were written to be sung.

100

Anton Webern / Alban Berg

Music for string quartet

The Alban Berg Quartet

Teldec 3984-21967-2; full price

In the decade prior to World War I a new artistic movement emerged in Germany, in which artists gave free rein to their innermost thoughts and feelings – in particular their fears and anxieties. With its emphasis on subjectivity, Expressionism, as it was called, can be seen as the final convulsive development of Romanticism. Although primarily a movement in the visual arts, the term Expressionism is also applied frequently to music, especially the music written between 1909 and approximately 1924 by Schoenberg and his two most devoted followers, Alban Berg and Anton Webern. It was in this period that their work made the final leap into atonality.

Webern's *Five Movements for String Quartet*, written in 1909 as an elegy for his mother, is a key work of this revolution. In place of the refined and civilized discourse of the traditional string quartet, we find terse, fragmented and often violent statements interspersed with moments of numbed stillness that suggest the terrible weariness of grief. One year later Berg's *String Quartet* – though less obviously disturbed than Webern's *Five Movements* – displays a similar rhythmic flexibility and a broad expressive range that is immediately apparent in the way the blunt opening statement quickly softens into a kind of question. There are moments of aching lyricism, but also bursts of fiery declamation, which – as in the Webern – often stretch the players' technique to breaking point. With the *Six Bagatelles for*

String Quartet (1911–13) Webern's musical language was refined to an even more aphoristic level. The entire work only lasts about four minutes and is permeated by a deep feeling of angst and impermanence.

In the end the complete freedom of atonality proved a conceptual dead end, and Schoenberg evolved his twelve-tone system (see p.144) as way of imposing some kind of structural framework on his material. Berg and Webern responded to the system in different ways. Berg's six-movement *Lyric Suite* for string quartet (1925–26) is immensely lyrical and expansive, still very much the product of a Romantic sensibility. Born out of Berg's doomed affair with a married woman, it is full of cryptic numerical symbolism and contains quotations from Zemlinsky's *Lyric Symphony* and Wagner's *Tristan and Isolde*. Its startling and dramatic changes of mood prompted the philosopher Theodor Adorno to describe the work as a "latent opera".

In contrast Webern's *String Quartet* is taut and highly structured. It was completed in 1938 as the Nazis occupied Austria (an event that Webern welcomed) and is a far cry from the emotional rawness and angularity of his early works for string quartet. The work grew from Webern's reflections on his daughter's pregnancy, and in the right hands there is a warm eloquence as well as astringency in its three movements. The music grows from the smallest seeds as Webern manipulates rhythm, tempo and duration into mercurial patterns that shift ceaselessly.

There is no doubt that Webern's intense and compacted works make difficult listening despite their brevity. Yet they are not, as some critics would have it, merely arid intellectual exercises – as is clear from this excellent CD, which features all of the pieces mentioned above. The Alban Berg Quartet's long familiarity with the music of both composers means that there is a confidence and an expressive vigour to their playing that is often lacking in less experienced interpreters. There's an almost breathless excitement to their performance of Berg's *Lyric Suite*, while their account of Webern's *String Quartet* tempers the formal precision with a warmly generous tone.